Buy High, Sell Higher

a profitable, momentum strategy

Tony Pow

Why you want to buy this book

It should improve your financial health substantially. There are about a million investment books. Why we need another one?

- Besides my original ideas, I select proven ideas from more than 100 books. I also include links to current articles that will bring more depth to the topic. This book has over 85 pages.

- A best seller was written by a young writer whose main income was from his books and none from his investing. His book is good for beginners or you want to brush up your English. Most of my incomes are from investing.

- Many popular books claiming the authors making millions. However, usually their techniques are hard to follow. Many admitted they had been bankrupted many times. Hence, their chance of bankrupting again is very high. Is bankruptcy fine with you? I cannot afford bankruptcy past and present. My techniques minimize risking my money.

- There are many popular books. They worked very well at one time and folks making millions following the advices. However, look at their recent performances of the last five years. Most of them cannot even beat the S&P 500 index.

- Check the recent mediocre performance of gurus such as Buffett. They are the market and they cannot beat themselves. Their techniques may no longer work.

- The average performance of the hedge fund is terrible. You cannot depend on others to invest for you.

- My credential. Here are my articles written in Seeking Alpha, an investment site.
  Amazing Return, A Tale of Two Portfolios and My Amazing Quarter.

Contents

Why you invest

You need to learn about investing sooner or later in your life. You need to take some calculated risks.

Compare the returns of the following assets: cash, CDs, treasury bills, bonds, real estate and stocks. We start with the risk-free investments and end with the riskiest. It turns out that the average returns are in the opposite order. Cash and CDs are not risk-free as inflation eats our profits. For example, the real return is negative for the 2% return in a CD and a 3% inflation rate. In addition you have to pay taxes for the 'returns'. Our capitalist system punishes us for not taking risk.

There are two kinds of risk: blind risk and calculated risk. If you buy a stock due to a recommendation from a commentator on TV or a tip, most likely you are taking a blind risk. It would be the same in buying a house without thoroughly evaluating the house and its neighborhood. When you buy stocks with a proven strategy (i.e. when/what stocks to buy and when/what stocks to sell), you are taking a calculated risk. In the long run, stocks with calculated and educated risks are profitable.

Be a turtle investor by investing in value stocks and holding for longer time periods (a year or more). "Buy and Monitor" is better an approach than "Buy and Hold" as some could lose all the stock values such as in the failure of Enron.

For experienced investors, shorting, short-term trading and covered calls would make you good profits. Simple market timing would reduce your losses during market down turns. If you buy a market ETF and use my simple market timing, you should have beaten the market by a wide margin from 2000 to 2019.

With so many frauds and poor management, do not trust anyone with your investing. Do not buy investing instruments that are highly marketed such as annuity and term insurance.

If you are a handy man and do not mind to satisfy the constant requests of your tenants, buy real estate in growing areas could be very profitable in the long run. Take advantage of the tax laws such as investing in a 401K especially the part that is matched by your company and/or a Roth IRA.

#Filler: 12 noon is not 12 pm
The Chinese restaurant I went to says they open at 12 am. Are they wrong or the world is wrong?

The next hour from 11 am is 12 am, NOT 12 pm. The one who set it up did it totally wrong and no one complains until now. If I were born earlier, I would have corrected it. If I were born here, I would be the president and every one would have a job by now.

Amazing returns

Amazing Returns

To achieve a consistent 10% return above S&P 500 over many years is every fund manager's dream. To double one's investment above the S&P500 return is amazing while tripling it is unheard of. I beat the S&P500 by 700% and I can detail the history of my transactions.

Many analysts show their average yearly returns and/or their returns of their top 10 stocks this time of year. The market has closed early today on Christmas Eve, so I have the time to check my recent performance. As a trader with many trades, it would be far too complicated for me to do the same for the entire year. I selected all the stocks I purchased in the last 90 days. Most of them are deeply-valued stocks. Let's check how I performed so far on these stocks.

Whenever you have achieved a high return such as this one, take the profit as it may have reached its peaks. To me, most profits are made in swing trades with an average holding period of just 90 days.

Stocks bought and their returns as of 12/25/12

Stocks	Date Bought	Return	SPY Return
BANR	12/07/12	3%	-.13%
KTCC	12/06/12	0%	.7%
QCOR	12/07/12	15%	-.1%
KTCC	12/06/12	-1%	.7%
ACTV	12/05/12	-5%	.7%
IAG	12/05/12	-1%	.7%
ADES	12/04/12	6%	.6%
NC	12/03/12	15%	-.3%
VELT	12/03/12	64%	-.3%
ANR	11/28/12	33%	4.8%
AAPL	11/16/12	1%	4.8%
C	11/14/12	13%	3.0%
DECK	11/13/12	16%	2.7%
MSFT	11/13/12	0%	2.7%
ALU	11/13/12	38%	2.7%
DLTR	11/09/12	7%	3.4%
CAT	11/08/12	4%	1.9%
MSFT	11/07/12	-8%	.5%
BSX	10/24/12	14%	.3%

BSX	10/19/12	7%	.3%
20			
AVG:		11%	1.35%

Beat SPY (in %) = (11%-1.35%)/1.35% = 716% or 7 times

Average Return = averaging each return of 20 stocks = 11%
Average Annualized Return = 148% or 122% (= 11% *365 / avg. holding period)
Average Return = Profit / Capitalization = 10%[1]

How the returns are calculated

Using BANR to illustrate how the return and the SPY return are calculated.

BANR	12/07/12	3%	-.13%

BANR was bought on 12/07/12 (17 days from 12/24/12) at 27.93 and it was at 30.43 on 12/24/12.
Rate of Return = (30.43 − 27.93) / 27.93 = 3%

SPY was at 142.53 on 12/07/12 and at 142.35 on 12/24/12.
  Rate of Return = (142.35-142.53) / 142.53 = -.13%

Commissions and dividends are not included for simplicity. Commissions are negligible and dividends could add about another 2% for the annual returns.

Interpreting the performance results

The quantity of each stock bought is not important as I am comparing the return of the stock. However, a few stocks have been listed twice as I bought two times usually on separate dates. If I chose them as one purchase instead of two, my return would appear even better. The purchases are real, so the amount of each stock is not identical to each other.

I'm not too excited yet. This phenomenal return could be just this one time only. 90 days is a short period. Consistency could be achieved with an improved stock picking technique, plain luck or a combination. By any measure, it is an extremely decent return. However, I do not expect beating S&P 500 by 7 times again.

My best return is from 2009 in my largest taxable account. It was over 80% beating the SPY by about 3 times. 2003 is another good year for profit. These two years are defined by me as the Early Recovery stage in a market cycle and the market provides the best profit opportunity.

The four losers are MSFT (-8%), ACTV (-5%), KTCC (-1%) and IAG (-1%). The best winners are: VELT (64%), ALU (38%), ANR (33%) and QCOR (19%). The following are in a 14% to 16% range: DECK, NC and BSX (2 purchases). Click here for the entire list.

Cheating the results

I could 'cheat' for better results by doing the following, but I did not:

1. Exclude stocks only purchased in last 20 days (instead of 15).

2. If my purchases of CSCO were included, the result would be even better. CSCO has been bought three times on 7/24/12 and it has gained 31% as of 12/25/12. I still have CSCO, but it is not included as it just hit the 90-days requirement.

3. I could include those buy orders that had not been executed due to their fast appreciation.

Hence, there are many ways to cheat, so you should read others' results carefully.

What stocks were included

There were 20 purchases. I bought some stocks twice and that counted as two purchases. None of the stocks have been sold as of 12/25/12. I have excluded the stocks that I am testing a strategy by trading them every month and most are in a separate account.

How the stocks were picked

The majority of the stocks were screened by my selected screens that had been proven profitable in the last 3 to 6 months, or are historically profitable at this stage of the market cycle. I also analyzed most of the screened stocks and assigned a score (15 and higher is a buy) based on the metrics that had a reliable predication recently. I do not stick with the scoring system 100% of the time, but most of them stocks that I purchased twice have high scores.

The poor performers were scored as: MSFT with a score of 13, ACTV 16, KTCC 27 and IAG 23. The scoring system is OK. MSFT should not be bought judging from its low score. However, I believe MSFT has a long-term appreciation potential. The other three are the latest purchases in this portfolio and they may perform better in a longer period of time.

The winners were scored as: VELT 34, ALU was not scored, ANR was not scored and QCOR 30. The scoring system is great for this group. ALU and ANR were selected from two Seeking Alpha articles and their selections were not based on these scores. I read several Wall Street Journal articles on ALU and CSCO to convince myself to buy both of them.

The average winners were scored as follows: DECK 9, NC 26 and BSX was not scored. DECK was selected based on an article from Seeking Alpha and it seemed DECK was experiencing the same short squeeze as CROX once did. BSX was selected from a Sunday paper article.

Observations

1. I notice that most big winners (ALU is $1) have a stock price less than $10. The myth of holding quality stocks with prices higher than $15 is not true here as most of my big winners were below $10 including ALU.

2. I did not double my normal purchases on VELT and ALU, which both turned out to be my best performers. VELT scored high in my analysis. ALU was very convincing but it seemed to be risky. 'Nothing risk and nothing gained' applies here. I did triple my

purchase on CSCO, which is a large company with good fundamentals that were not yet 'discovered' by the market.

Both AAPL and DECK gained more than 25% and then lost most of their gains during my short holding period. I should have sold AAPL as many of my fellow investors sold the winners expecting higher capital gains taxes next year. The myth of 'buy and hold' does not work here.

3. During this period, I had several buy orders that were not executed due to their rising stock prices. Market orders could be the solution. It is another example of pennies smart and a pound foolish.

4. It will be interesting to check the results again in 6 and 12 months. Except ALU, all are in my taxable accounts and I usually keep them for a year to qualify for the lower tax rates due to capital gains.

5. I have not described any specific method, but these concepts help you to build better strategies to customize to your individual situations and/or market conditions. Invest the money you can afford to lose. Past performance does not guarantee future results.

6. Reading articles such as Seeking Alpha can be beneficial providing they are not 'bump-and-switch' scheme. However, you should do your own analysis. It is your money after all.

7. The market has been up by .8% in the last 90 days and this portfolio increased by 11%. If my portfolio amplifies the market, I wonder whether it will be down by the same rate in a down market.

8. This portfolio is quite diversified even that I have not planned that way except weighing more with high tech companies. There are no big winners and no big losers that could change the average returns.

9. I tried not to include emerging countries such as China as I do not trust their balance sheets.

10. I have never achieved such an amazing return. I'm emotionally detached to big wins and big losses. It could be plain luck. Even the best strategy will have its "black swan" moment eventually.

11. To achieve over 100% annualized return is not sustainable by checking the top performers of the S&P 500 index and their returns. However, it is possible but not likely if you churn your portfolio more than once and you time the market correctly.

12. Time to take profits as most stocks here have achieved my objectives. Use the cash to buy stocks with a similar appreciation potential. You will never go broke taking profits.

Conclusion

My three steps of making a stock purchase are: 1. Market timing, 2. Screening stocks, 3. Stock Analysis and 4. When and what to sell. They have all been discussed throughout the book. Market timing and strategy (#2 and #3) does not always work, but it will go better with using them.

I am the living proof *against* the Efficiency Theory and the claims that stock picking does not work. It may not work from time to time, but in the long run it works.

Footnote

[1] Profit / Capitalization should be a little less than 20%. The original 10% is correct when you invest all the 20 stocks at the start of the beginning of the investment period. I bought these stocks on different dates. If I assume the average time of all the stock purchases is at a mid-point, then my average capitalization is only half and hence giving a 20% return.

It is slightly less than 20% as I did not include the stocks that I bought in the last 15 days. Use the number for a comparison and that's why we have to be concerned with the performance from most investment subscriptions.

Introduction

My close friend has similar income as I. When we retired (I retired at least 10 years earlier), I had about four times his total equity. The main reason is I followed the time-honored "Buy Low, Sell High" strategy and supplemented with this "Buy high, Sell Higher".

Before 2000, market timing is a waste of time. Since then, it is critical to your financial health. The average loss of the last two market crash is about 45%. My simple technique described in this book does not require any charting or any subscription/tool. It does not detect the peaks and bottoms but it would have saved you a lot of money in exiting and reentering the market. Most likely it will detect the next crash. As in life, nothing is guaranteed.

The book shows you to find growth and evaluate stocks in term of the short-term appreciation potential. Growth stocks change fundamentals every quarter (3 months). Ensure you have stop loss order to protect your profit. I prefer to adjust the stop orders when the stocks appreciate.

Do not marry with a stock. When the fundamentals change or your objective has been fulfilled, you need to sell it.

How this book is organized

This book is divided into sections.

Some graphs cannot be displayed adequately on a small screen of an e-reader. Kindle is available in the current version of Windows, so you can read e-books on your larger screen of your PC. Most graphs are in landscape orientation for both paperback and e-reader format.

A link is usually included for these screens. Copy it to your browser to display the graphs on your PC. Instructions on how to produce some graphs are provided as you should try them out. One example is how to produce a chart on detecting market crashes.

It is easier to display the graphs and tables in landscape mode, which can be selectable in your e-reader.

The font size and page size of most e-book formats can be adjusted. The special character is a "smiling face" that the current Kindle does not convert correctly.

There are clickable links to web articles. Most of them are from my own web sites and public web sites such as Wikipedia. Some public links may not be available in the future as they are not under my control.

Fidelity Video provides video clips to explain some basic terms and it may require Fidelity customers to sign on in order to view them. Check the trial offer from Fidelity. YouTube offers similar video lessons.

These links extend the usefulness of this book by making available specific topics that may not be interesting to every reader.

The paperback readers. Most important links are provided, so you can enter the link into your browser.

Get the same information by entering a search in Wikipedia such as Market Timing.

Investopedia is another source beside Wikipedia.
http://www.investopedia.com/

'Afterthoughts' includes my additional comments and comments from others. Readers can make comments in this book's website. These comments may be included in the Afterthoughts in subsequent revisions, with the commenter's last name redacted. It is for freer and informal discussion on the topic. In addition, it provides the name of my book for the related topic.

For convenience, this book uses SPY, an Exchange Traded Fund (ETF) simulating S&P 500, as the benchmark for the market.

Annualized returns (Return * 365 / (Days in between)) are used where appropriate for more meaningful comparison. To illustrate, I have a 10% return in 6 months, a 10% in a year and a 10% in 2 years. It is more meaningful to use annualized returns of 20%, 10% and 5% respectively in this example.

Usually I do not include the dividend in calculating returns, so you can add an estimated 1.5% to the annualized return. In addition, compounding is usually not used for easier calculation, so the actual positive return should be better.

About the author

I graduated from Cal. State University at San Jose in Industrial Engineering and University of Mass. in Amherst with a MS in Industrial Engineering. My last job was in IT. I have been an investor for over 30 years.

Dedication
To all retail investors and future retail investors including my grandchildren.

I sincerely hope this book and my other books will build bridges with fellow investors with different backgrounds.

Acknowledgement

Thanks to Seeking Alpha, Wikipedia and Investopedia for the many helpful links to enrich this book.

Yahoo!Finance and Finviz.com for the tools and charts used in this book.

Important notices

Version	Paperback	eBooks
1.0	07/15	07/15
2.2	06/20	06/20
2.4	11/21	11/21

Printed version. ISBN-13: 978-1514852996 ISBN-10: 1514852993

Book store managers can order the paper version of this book from Createspace.com.
https://tonyp4idea.blogspot.com/2020/12/book-managers.html

Book update.
https://ebmyth.blogspot.com/2020/12/updates-for-all-books.html

For beginners

If I explained every investing term, this book would be at double in size and will be boring for most readers. However, I provide the following links for beginners.

Read basic investment articles for beginners. Both Fidelity and AAII (both require being a client or a member) have excellent articles. Alternatively, buy a book for beginners. To include all the basic terms and concepts, I have to double the size of this book which is already lengthy and bore most readers who already have the basic knowledge.

Click here for Morningstar classroom.
http://morningstar.com/cover/classroom.html
Click here for Vanguard.
https://investor.vanguard.com/investing/investor-education
Click here for Investopedia's Tutorials.
http://www.investopedia.com/university/
Click here for Yahoo!
http://finance.yahoo.com/education/begin_investing
Click here for Fidelity basic in investing.
https://www.fidelity.com/investment-guidance/investing-basics

---

money. Do not trade without doing due diligence and be warned that most data may be obsolete. All my articles and the associated data are for informational and illustration purposes only. I'm not a professional investment counselor, a tax professional or any other field. Seek one before you make any investment decisions. Remember to consult with a registered financial adviser before making any investment decisions. The above mentioned also applies for all other advice such as on accounting, taxes, health and any topic mentioned in this book. Tax laws change all the time, so talk to your tax advisors before taking any action. Most of the time, I use annualized for a better comparison; 5% in a month is more than 4% in a year for example. For simplicity, most of my returns do not include commissions, exchange fees, order spread and dividends. It is the same for all the links contained in this book. Some articles may offend some one or some organization unintentionally. If I did, I'm sorry about that. I am politically and religiously neutral. I have provided my best efforts to ensure the accuracy of my articles. Data also from different sources was believed to be accurate. However, there is no guarantee that they are accurate and suitable for the current market conditions and /or your individual situations. The values of some parameters such as RSI(14) are arbitrarily set by me. My publisher and I are not liable for any damages in using this book or its contents. I do not own trademarks of all the companies and products mentioned in this book.

1   My momentum performance

The following includes all the actual transactions from September, 2013 to Dec., 2013 in my momentum portfolio. "Lot Date" is the day I evaluate what stocks to buy. Some stocks are bought in different days after the evaluation and some are not bought. I am not responsible for any errors in preparing the following tables.

Lot Date	Stock	Buy Date	Days	Ann. %
09/04/13	BOFI	09/04/13	6	(175%)
	GMCR	09/04/13	14	110%
	Z	09/04/13	6	40%
	FB	09/05/13	8	419%
	AFOP	09/04/13	6	353%
	EGAN	09/04/13	5	194%
	PB	09/06/13	10	78%
09/11/13	ARWR	09/12/13	12	136%
	CATM	09/13/13	4	136%
	GILD	09/13/13	6	157%
	YELP	09/11/13	6	242%
	TRN	09/13/13	32	24%
09/24/13	AFOP	09/26/13	22	(105%)
	DRYS	09/24/13	81	15%
	PACB	09/28/13	20	(258%)
10/02/13	ZLC	10/02/13	14	293%
	FB	10/02/13	15	20%
10/05/13	DYAX	10/08/13	16	(109%)
	FSS	10/08/13	31	160%
10/18/13	GERN	10/18/13	21	1176%
	ALGN	10/22/13	48	(22%)
	COBZ	10/22/13	62	108%
	WAL	10/18/13	21	103%
	LCI	10/22/13	10	434%
	AKRX	10/31/13	15	334%
	BREW	11/01/13	7	194%
	BCEI	10/22/13	10	434%
	RAD	10/22/13	41	142%
11/05/13	LCC merged	11/06/13	3	639%
	TRN	11/08/13	63	41%
	CIR	11/05/13	43	21%
11/12/13	LCI	11/12/13	38	138%
	TRN	11/12/13	3	785%
	UBNT	11/12/13	3	1461%
	LCC	11/12/13	61	20%
	FCN	11/12/13	38	(12%)
11/19/13	FOE	11/19/13	35	(6%)

	NUVA	12/11/13	9	93%
11/25/13	GTN	12/03/13	3	1289%
	CRY	11/26/13	49	39%
	ARC	11/26/13	24	(85%)
	BONT	12/20/13	25	(344%)
12/03/13	AIRM	12/03/13	17	44%
	FIX	12/03/13	20	(97%)
12/10/13	MDXG	12/19/13	8	1162%
	MPAA	12/16/13	7	(7%)
	LBMH	12/14/13	6	627%
	UVE	12/11/13	12	48%
	USAK	12/10/13	13	(18%)
	ARC	12/10/13	13	(144%)
	CONN	12/12/13	11	55%
	REI	12/10/13	10	192%
		Biggest loss		(344%)
		Average		200%

My best profitable month

All the stocks purchased have been sold. Some stocks were bought twice in another account and they may have been in different prices/holding durations. Stopped this strategy in 2019 due to the risky market, but will return when the market is less risky. In 2019, I switched to shorting stocks. Jan., 2014 was one of my best months then.

Lot Date	Stock	Buy Date	Days	Ann. %
01/14/14	LCI	01/14/14	30	85%
	ENDP	01/16/14	42	140%
	LCI	01/14/14	38	208%
	NSTG	01/14/14	56	36%
	BABY	01/26/14	35	156%
	NSTG	01/14/14	59	34%
	ZNGX	01/21/14	31	133%
01/22/14	ANIP	01/22/14	29	195%
	KS	01/22/14	33	115%
	CHIP	01/22/14	19	246%
	SLXP	01/22/14	33	77%
	GMCR	01/22/14	20	743%
		Biggest loss		34%
		Average		181%

Explanation

- Lot Date. I usually group the stocks I buy by weeks. When I have losses two times in a row, I would buy fewer stocks or even skip purchase altogether.

I try to maintain a total balance for this portfolio. I would buy fewer stocks when the balance is close to this threshold. As of 3/15/14, the market is too risky (plunging or peaking), and hence I would not buy any momentum stocks. When the market falls, these momentum stocks will fall faster and steeper than the rest of the market.

- I started this momentum portfolio far earlier, but I only recorded it recently. I took a long summer break in 2013 and resumed it in September, 2013 (the start date of the first table).

  There are some positions not sold after Dec., 2013. Anyway, I have enough data for illustration purposes. Most likely, the reason for showing any 'unclosed' positions is due to housekeeping errors, not trying to present a better result than what may appear.

- I did not include the stocks that have not been bought due to my lower buy prices and/or not meeting my criteria of what to buy. When any of my subscription services tells me the stock is not a buy, I skip it. A few times, some recommended stocks just skyrocketed in prices in the open. I did not buy most if not all of these stocks.

- I've averaged the returns for the above tables. The first table has 200% annualized return while the second one has 181%.

  However, the actual profit of this portfolio is far better in the second table – most likely due to some larger position sizes. The higher annualized return in the first table is due to shorter durations. In my actual monitor, I ignore the returns if they are less than five days, as they distort the returns.

- The actual performance should be worse due to not considering the idle cash. I also exclude the contra ETFs to hedge the portfolio. In 2013, the hedging is a losing game in a rising market. Dividends are not considered in calculating the returns.

- The better way is to compare the performances with the S&P 500 index, which is too time-consuming for me.

- My holding period is short. With many exceptions, I sell these stocks within a month or they have appreciated a lot.

- You can have a portfolio for momentum stocks and another one for value stocks.

2   Herd theory

When the herd makes money, they think they're a genius. The last one to leave the herd will be the fool of all fools such as the last holders of Lehman Brothers, AIG, Bear Sterns, internet stocks in 2000, etc. The biggest fools are the 'value' buyers when these companies were plunging fast. When a specific stock looked great yesterday and it lost 50% today, it 'must' be super good to some. Wrong! Check out why it plunged. It could be missing some important metric, or something is really wrong with the company that did not show up in the research.

The real genius is the one who makes money all the way up, but leaves before the bubble bursts. Even a genius cannot predict the peak and the bottom, but I'll call him/her a genius if s/he is right better   than   60%   of   the   time.

Recently dividend growth stocks have the highest premium in the last 30 years. It is a mild bubble when we've many retired, or retiring folks seeking income. However, the bubble will burst when the interest rates rises. At that time, the long-term bonds with low yields will lose.

Dividend stocks will benefit when the interest rates is low. Bond holders would move to dividend stocks from their low-yield bonds. Long-term bonds lose their value when the interest rates rises, and vice versa.

It is the same for the internet bubble in 2000. I did unload most of my tech funds in early April, 2000. The more I read during that time, the more I got scared. It was partly luck and partly 'genius' to move all these sector funds to traditional industries. At that time, they did not have contra ETFs, so cash, money market fund and bonds would be the best choices.

3   Success in market correction in Oct., 2014

I bought the following 4 stocks from my taxable account during the Ebola panic in Oct., 2014. It was a correction. I placed the orders and took off on vacation. The results are:

Recent purchases	Return (as of 5-8-15)	Bought
AET	50%	10/15/14
STZ	42%	10/15/14
SWKS	95%	10/10/14
CI	50%	10/15/14

2015 and beyond

I am cautious this year but I will be very careful next year in timing the market. From my memory, we do not have a down year in a year before election including 2007. When the Fed hikes the interest rate, the market will fall like a deck of cards and it will be amplified by the record margin debt.

Many experts including a best seller tell their readers to abandon stocks, some as early as 2009. If you followed them, you would have lost all the profits from the recommendation date to now. My simple technique tells you to invest fully since September, 2009. I play corrections by buying during dips and selling during upswings. When the market plunges, sell everything. Usually the plunge takes longer than one year to reach the bottom. The average loss of the last two market plunge is about 45% and followed by the most profitable time to buy stocks.

Conclusion

Hope I have shared some of my investing ideas.

- The media amplifies the news. When the oil price is dropping, they just predict a higher loss in order to sell their stuffs.

- Selling a loser in a taxable account and buying it back in a retirement account avoids wash sale and take advantage of the tax loss.
- Invest in the sector that institution investors are dumping but select stocks with highest appreciation potential.
- Small stocks though risky have chance of larger appreciation especially those stocks no analyst follows. However, when the market starts to plunge, they should be the first ones to sell from my experiences.
- Chinese stocks are risky but they have been highly profitable in the last year.
- I prefer to churn my portfolio so I have better appreciation potential with newer info. If I do not sell, where can I get money to buy new stocks? One's strategy.
- Selling a stock does not mean you will not buy it back. We should be emotionally detached to any stock.
- Expect losses. Nothing risked, nothing gained. When the market is risky, reduce purchases and sell some stocks whose fundamentals have deteriorated.

The following is from my book "How to be a billionaire" and it is used to conclude this article.

"We come to this earth with nothing and leave with nothing. Why do we fight for wealth, prestige and power? However, if we do not have the objective for wealth, prestige and power, it is a life without meaning. In addition, money should not be our primary objective in life and happiness/health has to be earned and cannot be bought with money."

4   Trading by headlines

On 6/29/2019, Trump and Xi seemed to settle trade war in the G20. The market would likely rise on the coming Monday. Luckily I had closed a short position. Many chip stocks would rise as they can sell their products to Huawei. I have several of these stocks expecting the trade war would be settled. The farmers and their supporting industry would breathe easier.

I bet the shipping companies would be more profitable from the news. Without doing further research, I checked out this shipping sector and found the following stocks had been up more than 4%: DHT, NM, SBLK, STNG, TNK and ASC. It was during the weekend, so your trade account should be able to trade after hours and you need to act right after the news.

I exchanged comments with Andrew McElroy, a sector rotation expert. He does not have the rules set up as in this book but he makes great trades by 'seeing' the market and using technical analysis. The following is from his article.

"The idea is fairly simple. There is more potential for profit (and loss) in individual sectors, especially when the index is trading sideways. I try to buy strong sectors which have pulled back onto support and avoid overbought sectors at resistance. I also use Elliott Wave to identify cycles of buying and selling and stages in trends."

I would like to include headlines such as Trump's election, interest rates hikes and new regulations.

When it rains in Brazil, buy coffee futures

Recently it rained too much in SE Asia, so buy rice futures. I did not trade futures, so I missed out on the opportunity and unfortunately there is no equivalent ETF for rice. In the beginning of 2012, we should know the farming crops especially corn will not be good due to the flooding and drought in different parts of the world. Act accordingly for the profit potentials.

When a war is starting in the Middle East, most likely the oil price will rise. Buy the oil ETF and sell it when the chance of the war is reduced. Many tiny drops of profit could turn into a river of profit.

Trading by headlines is profitable, but it is hard to master and is very time-consuming. Test this strategy on paper for years before you commit real money as in most strategies. Most couch potatoes read the newspaper and watch TV all day long without making a penny. He could be couch potato millionaire if he read this article, paper traded/refined the strategy and acted on it!

However, the media tend to exaggerate headlines in order to sell their ads. Ignore all the recommendations on stocks. Most likely they are outdated information and some may be used to manipulate others. Do your own research as your mother taught you that there is no free lunch.

Rules of the game

1. Do not be too emotional; ignore your past wins and losses except when using them as lessons if they are valid (i.e. educated guesses).

2. Do not trade the entire farm. Consider option, ETFs and/or small trade on stocks, which have too many other factors to be considered.

3. Trade it fast – today's headlines will not be headlines tomorrow. There are very few exceptions.

4. Where there is a winner, there is always a loser. For example, Apple was a winner with the iPhone and BlackBerry was a loser. Same for Best Buy and Circuit City.

5. Ensure you can trade after hours from your broker.

6. Do not forget when to exit for either a small profit or a small loss.

7. Quick evaluation. The headline will be gone if you do not act fast. Skip companies with poor metrics such as high debt and low earnings yield. Prefer to buy an ETF related to the headline.

8. Most likely someone has used the information before you get it. However, some info can be deducted before it occurs. Insider purchases is a good guide.

9. I recommended crude oil at $30 per barrel in Jan. 15, 2016 as the price was at rock bottom. For value sectors, you may have to wait for a long time for the market to realize its value.

10. Sometimes you ignore stock evaluations as the headline news is more important. Learn my 5-minute evaluation process of a stock (a quick way but not recommended if you have time to do thorough research):
   - From Finviz.com, enter the stock or ETF symbol. Look at how many greens in metrics over reds.
   - Check out Forward P/E (E>0 and P/E < 20), Debut / Equity (< 50%) and P/FCF (not in red color).
   - SMA20 (or SMA50 for longer holding period). If SMA20 is > 10%, it is trending up.
   - Scroll down for Insider Trade. It usually is a good buy if insiders are buying recently and heavily with market prices.
   - Be cautious on foreign and low-volume stocks.
   - If most of the above are positive, it is likely a buy. As in life, nothing is 100% certain.

If you have a hard time following the above, most likely this strategy is not for you and it is better to return to your couch. No offense.

Volatile market and headlines

As of 7/2012 (2015 too and historically a positive market in a year right before the election), the market went sideways and was influenced by headlines. 2013 had been volatile with dips and surges influenced by daily news. The trend was up though. The Federal debt problem, EU crisis... had not been resolved. Every time we had good news, the market rose, and vice versa. In this market, buy on dips (3% down from last temporary peak) and sell on temporary surges

(3% up from last temporary bottom). Some use 5% instead of 3% depending on one's risk tolerance.

Trend and calendar timing

Usually following the trend is better than ignoring it.

- Many retail investors want to get rid of the losers for year-end tax planning. Buy them at year-end and sell them early next year. In the year end of 2012, it acted the opposite as folks were selling their winners expecting a larger tax bite next year but that turned out to be false.

  This could be the reason for a sell-off of Apple in year-end of 2012 and it gave us a good entry point. To me, Apple's fundamentals were sound though the media said otherwise. In a few months, Apple became a value stock from a growth stock according to the press.

- Investors are not rational and follow the market blindly. The strategy 'Buy low and sell high' works.

- We have so much good news and bad news in the same year. Ensure the bad news will not extend to worse news. Timing is everything. Buy on bad news and sell on good news; it does not work when the market plunges.

- The media influences the market. Analyze their arguments. If they exaggerate them, do the opposite.

- Over-reaction to earnings missed or gained. When the company missed the earnings by 5%, there is a very good chance the stock will be down in a year, and vice versa. However, when it missed by 1% and the stock lost by 10%, it could be a buying opportunity, particularly when it was a temporary condition and the company is fundamentally sound.

- Buy the stock at dip when a solvable problem surfaces. Sell after the problem has been resolved. Ceiling debt is such a solvable problem and it is caused by politics. In the beginning of 2013, I mentioned that the debt problem had not been resolved and we would have this ceiling debt problem periodically until it will be eventually resolved.

Scheduled events

Some events are scheduled such as earnings announcements, unemployment reports, etc. Most likely educated guesses of the outcomes have already been circulated in the web.

The last five events on the Federal debt handling (using fancy names such as sequester and debt ceiling) were scheduled such as the government shutdown. They drove the market down by about an average of 5% each time. Sell before the event and buy back afterward. The Congress has cancelled these debt deadlines as of 1/2014.

Many sectors are impacted by events such as Trump's success in election, hikes of interest rates and trade wars.

Follow the institutional investors

They drive the market. When they see the sector is over-valued or the peak has been reached, they rotate sectors.

Use deduction

In 2014, China has a great harvest on wheat, corn and rice. China's population is #1 in the world and its middle class is growing. The farmers in the US will be hurt as they cannot export these products to their number one customer. Use the same logic to deduct that there will be problems in the companies that supply products and services to the farmers. They are combines, fertilizer companies and seed companies. It further translates into Deere, Potash, Monsanto and AGCO.

Due to increasing wealth in 2017, Chinese demanded more meat. It takes a lot of corn to produce one pound of meat and in turn corn needed fertilizers. Hence, you can expect the companies producing fertilizers will increase their profits.

Geopolitical crisis

Many times no action is the best action. It applies here. I had my experience in selling too many stocks via stops in 911. The market returned in a few days and I did not buy them back.

An analysis from Ned David Research covers 51 events from 1900 to 2014. My interpretation for actions: Trade the affected sector (via sector ETF) in the first few days and reverse the trade 2 months after. Many times it means the oil price and gold price would rise.

I bought SH (a contra ETF to SPY) in August, 2017 as August and September are statistically the worst months in addition to the high risk in the current market. It is expected to be sold on Nov. 1. The North Korea crisis did not do much to the market on the first day but the market (the S&P 500) lost 1.45% and the risky NASDAQ lost 2.13% (see my blog on FAANG) on the second day.

If there is a hint of war or conflict, buy gold (GLD, gold trusts and gold coins) and defense stocks such as Northrop Grumman (NOC), L3 (LHX), Raytheon (RTN) and Lockheed Martin (LMT). I stayed away from Boeing (BA) in early 2020. If the conflict may disrupt oil transportation and/or production, buy oil such as (OIL and USO) and oil stocks.

Caveat. Need to understand the crisis. If it would lead to World War 3, most sectors will not recover for a long while. Again, there is no sure thing in investing otherwise there would be no poor folks. However, educated guesses should materialize more often than not.

My experiences
- When the interest rates is expected to rise, plan on investments that are favorable to it and vice versa.
- On the same week, CROX lost almost 40% in one day. I bought some and made about 10% profit in a week. CROX's fundamentals were no good and it did have a history of a roller coaster ride in its stock price. After a year, I found out that I sold it too early as the stock price doubled. Better to buy a stock on its way up than down unless we identify that the bottom has been reached.

- I was on vacation while the second incident of the Boeing Max happened. Should have shorted the stock. In addition, Boeing's suppliers would suffer too similar to Apple's suppliers on Apple.

  https://www.barrons.com/articles/boeing-737-max-jet-production-cut-suppliers-stocks-51554499957?siteid=yhoof2&yptr=yahoo

- I missed applying the same trick to the rise of Apple when Apple announced its new iPod. I should at least buy the stocks of its part suppliers. I hope learn from this lesson and take advantage of future similar circumstances.
  I missed the opportunity to buy uranium stocks. It should be bought after Japan's disaster. When Japan approved the reopening of nuclear reactors today, these stocks including CCJ, DNN, LEU, URRE, UEC, URZ, URG and UUUU surge. When China's new nuclear reactors are on-line, they will surge again.
- Experiences in early 2014.
  Recently and in a short time, I made a good profit on BBY and a tiny profit on TGT. Both were bought due to headlines.

Section I: Simple techniques

Introduction

For starters, just trade ETFs such as SPY (an ETF simulating the market), and you can skip the rest of the book. It only takes a few minutes every month. When the market is not plunging, buy or keep SPY (or any ETF that stimulates the market); otherwise sell it. Do the opposite when the market is recovering.

If you have less than $50,000 to invest, just buy ETFs. Improve your investing skills by reading investment articles from this book and your broker's website. For example, Fidelity has a lot of information for investors.

Subscription to AAII is recommended. When your portfolio grows more than $50,000, invest on a subscription such as Value Line, GuruFocus, Zacks or IBD (more for momentum traders). Initially, use the information for paper trading on value stocks, which is usually available from brokers.

For the long term, knowledge is most important in your investing life and experience comes next. Retail investors have a lot of advantages over fund managers. However, I advise you NOT to be a trader. Hence, you should ignore the 'fabulous' trade systems that claim to be very profitable. Statistically most amateur traders lose money as they cannot compete with experienced, disciplined traders.

How to start

I recommend trading ETFs first and when the market is not risky. The very basic terms such as ETF are not fully explained here; try Investopedia for terms you need to know. Otherwise this book would be doubled in size and it would bore most readers. Investopedia, your broker's website (especially Fidelity) and AAII (requiring subscription) provide many excellent articles. Alternatively, buy a book for beginners. Here are some freebies:

Click here for Morningstar classroom.
http://morningstar.com/cover/classroom.html
Click here for Vanguard.
https://investor.vanguard.com/investing/investor-education
Click here for Investopedia's Tutorials.
http://www.investopedia.com/university/
Click here for Yahoo!
http://finance.yahoo.com/education/begin_investing
Click here for Fidelity basic in investing.
https://www.fidelity.com/investment-guidance/investing-basics

1   Simplest market timing

Why market timing

Before 2000, market timing was a waste of time. However after that, we have had two market plunges with the average loss of about 45%. It sounds harder to time the market than it actually is. We have a simple technique to detect market plunges and when to reenter the market. Our objective is reducing the loss to 25%.

Market timing depends on charts; the following describes how to use chart information without creating charts. Most charts will not identify the peaks and bottoms of the market as they depend on data (i.e. the stock prices). However, it would reduce further losses. It is simpler than it sounds. Just follow the procedure below.

The first part of this technique detects market plunges, and the second part advises you when to reenter the market. It applies to individual stocks too. It also works to detect the trend of a sector (entering an ETF for the specific sector instead of SPY) and a specific stock.

How to detect market plunges without charts (a.k.a. **Death Cross**)
1. Bring up Finviz.com.

2. Enter SPY (or any ETF that simulates the market) or RSP for equally weighed SPY.

3. If SMA-200% is positive, it indicates that the market plunge has not been detected and you can skip the following steps.

4. The market is plunging if SMA-50% is more negative than SMA-200%. To illustrate this condition, SMA-200% is -2% and SMA-50% is -5%.

5. Sell most stocks starting with the riskiest ones first such as the ones with negative earnings, high P/Es and/or high Debt/Equity. Obtain this info from Finviz.com by entering the symbol of the stock you own.

6. Conservative investors should sell only those overpriced stocks. Aggressive investors should sell all stocks. Extremely aggressive investors should sell all stocks, buy contra ETFs, and even short stocks. I do not recommend beginners to be aggressive.

When to return to the market (a.k.a. Golden Cross)

Use the above in a reversed sense to detect whether the market has been recovering. However, when the SMA-200% turns positive, I would start buying value stocks (low P/E but the 'E' has to be positive, and/or low Debt/Equity).

1. Bring up Finviz.com.
2. Enter SPY (or any ETF that simulates the market).
3. If SMA-200% is negative, the market is not recovering, and you can skip the following steps.
4. Sell all contra ETFs and close all shorts if you have any.
5. Market recovery is confirmed when SMA-50% is more positive than SMA-200%. To illustrate this condition, SMA-200% is 2% and SMA-50% is 5%. Commit a large percent of cash (or all cash for aggressive investors) to stocks. If you do not know what to buy, buy SPY or an ETF that simulates the market.

How often to check the market timing indicators
Do the above once a month. When the SPY price is closer to SMA actions percentage, perform the above once a week. The charts and data for market timing described in this book are based on SMA-350 (Simple Moving Average) that is more preferable than this simple procedure, but it requires some simple charting.

Nothing is perfect
If the market timing is perfect, there would be no poor folks. The major 'defects' are:

- It does not detect the peak / bottom as it depends on past data. However, it would save you a lot during the crash.
- It is hard to determine whether it is a correction or a crash.
- From 2000 to 2010, there was only one false signal. The indicator tells you to exit and then tells you to reenter the market shortly. In most cases, you do not lose a lot. After 2010, we have more false signals.
- The market may not be rational or may be influenced due to specific conditions such as excessive printing of USD. If you do not mind charting, use SMA 350 (or 400) using SPY. Buy when the price is above SMA-350 (or SMA-400), and sell otherwise. SMA-400 reduces the number of false signals, but it is not nimble.

2   Quick analysis of ETFs

Evaluate an ETF

ETFs are a basket of stocks according to the market, a specific sector, country or a specific theme.

Yahoo!Finance used to give the P/E of an ETF. Try to get it from ETFdb.com. Enter the symbol of the ETF such as XLU, and then select Valuation. If it is below 15 and above zero, it could be a value ETF. Also, if the current price is lower than its NAV, it is sold at a discount (or premium vice versa). Compare its YTD Return to SPY's.

Alternatively, get similar info from http://www.multpl.com/. In addition, this website provides the following metrics: Shiller P/E, Price/Sales, and Price/Book.

From Finviz.com, enter the ETF symbol. If SMA-20%, SMA-50% and SMA-200% are all positive, most likely the ETF is in an uptrend. To illustrate, SMA-200 is Simple Moving Average for the last 200 trading sessions (no trading on weekends and specific holidays). The percent is how much the stock price of the ETF is above the SMA. If the percent is negative, it means the stock price is below the SMA.

If your average holding period of your stocks is about 50 days, SMA-50% is more appropriate to you.

If RSI(14) > 65, it is probably oversold; if it is < 30, it is probably under-sold (indicating value).

In addition, ensure the ETF's average volume is high (I suggest more than 10,000 shares), the market cap is more than 300 M, and it has low fees. Most popular ETFs have these characteristics. Beginners should avoid leveraged ETFs.

How to determine if the sector has been recovered

It is easier to profit by following the uptrend of an ETF using the above info. It is hard to detect when the bottom of an ETF has been reached. If SMA-20%, SMA-50% and SMA-200% are all positive, most likely the ETF is in an uptrend or it has recovered. It does not always happen as predicted, so use stops to protect your investment.

An example

First, determine whether the market is risky. Most beginners should not invest in a risky market. Advanced investors can bet against the market or a specific sector by buying contra ETFs or puts.

Next, you want to limit the number of sector ETFs by selecting those that are either in an uptrend or hitting bottom (bottom is hard to predict). Personally I prefer sectors with long-term uptrends (indicated by articles found in many websites including cnnfn.com and Seeking Alpha.

For illustration purposes only for deteriorating market conditions, I would select the following ETFs: SPY (simulating the market based on large companies) and XLP (consumer staples). XLP should perform better than XLY (consumer discretionary) during a recession as those products are the necessities.

Technical indicators such as SMA-50 (Simple Moving Average for the last 50 sessions), SMA-200 and RSI(14) are obtained from Finviz.com and the rest are obtained from Yahoo!Finance.com. After you buy the ETF, use a stop loss to protect your investment. For example, biotech sector moved up for many months until it crashed in 2015. Change the stop loss value every month to protect your gains in this case.

As of 2/5/2016	SPY	XLP (staples)	XLY (discret.)
Price	190	50	71
NAV	192	50	73
• **Technical**			
SMA-50	-4%	0%	-7%
SMA-200	-6%	2%	-7%
RSI(14)	44	50	36
Other	Double bottom at $186		
• **Fundamental**			
P/E	17	20	19
Yield	2.1%	2.5%	1.5%
YTD return	-5%	0.5%	-5%
Net asset	174 B	9 B	10 B

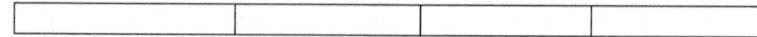

Explanation

- The figures may not be identical among websites due to the dates they are using.
- XLY has the best discount among the 3 ETFs as most investors believe a recession is coming.
- XLP has less down trend among the 3 ETFs as expected.
- XLY is more undersold among the three as expected.
- Double bottom is a technical pattern that indicates the stock would surge upward.
- SPY has a better value according to its P/E.
- XLY's dividend is the least among the three as they have more tech companies in the ETF. They have to plow back the profits to research and development.
- XLP has the best YTD return among the three.
- As long as the asset is above 500 M (200 M for specialized ETFs), it is fine and all three pass this mark.

There are many metrics such as Debt/Equity not readily available from most websites. Many sites list the top holdings of a specific ETF. Just average the metrics of the top ten or so of its stock holdings.

#Filler: Illogical logic

If we do not test for the pandemic, we would have zero increase in this pandemic. Some silly folks buy this argument. What happens to the once-great country?

An example

This example evaluates RING, a gold miner, using ETFdb and Finviz that are free from the web. The data is from July, 6, 2020.

Bring up ETFdb and enter RING in the search. There are basic info that are important to me: Sector (gold miners), Asset Size (Large-Cap), Issuer (iShares), Inception (Jan. 31, 2012), Expense Ratio (0.39%) and Tax Form (1099).

They fit all my requirements. The expense ratio is higher than most ETFs that simulate an index such as SPY. I try to trade ETFs using Tax Form 1099 in my taxable accounts. The large cap created about 8 years ago by a reputable company is good.

Select "Dividend and Valuation". P/E of 17.39 is fine in a rank of 11 in 27 in a similar group of ETFs. As in my books, I stated it is hard to evaluate miners. I buy this ETF primarily to fight the possibility of inflation and the potential depreciation of USD. The dividend rate of 0.52% (0.70% from Finviz) is in the low range of the scale; it is fine for me as dividend is not my concern.

There is more info from this website. For simplicity, bring up Finviz:
- The short-term trend is up (SMA-20% = 8% and SMA-50% = 7%).
- The long-term trend is up (SMA-200% = 26%).
- It is close to overbought (RSI(14) = 64%; 65% to me is overbought).
- It is -4% from 52-w High. It has performed well from the YTD, Last Year, Last Quarter, Last Month and Last Week.
- It almost doubled in price from mid-March this year.
- Avg. Vol. is fine.

From ETFdb, check the Holding. It has 39 stocks, so it is quite diversified for this industry. The two top holdings are NEM (19%) and ABX (18%), which is listed as GOLD in NYSX. I also consider buyiing these two stocks in addition to RING. You can estimate the other metrics that are not available by averaging these two stocks. Here is my summary:

STOCK	NEM	GOLD
Forward P/E	20	25
Debt / Share	0.31	0.24
ROE	17%	22%
Sales Q/Q	43%	30%
EPS Q/Q	389%	254%
SMA50	2%	4%

RSI(14)	59%	60%
Insider Trans	-13%	N/A
Fidelity's Equity Summary Score	6.1	6.8

3   Rotate four ETFs

We can beat the market by rotating one ETF that represents the market such as SPY and cash via market timing. Aggressive investors can add SH or PSQ (contra ETFs) to the four to have better returns during market plunges.

During a market uptrend, rotating the following four ETFs could be more profitable than staying with SPY (or any ETF that simulates the market). Be warned that a short-term capital gain in taxable accounts is not treated as favorably as the long-term capital gain; check current tax laws.

The allocation percentages depend on your individual risk tolerance. You can use indexed mutual funds. Compare their expenses and restrictions. Some mutual funds charge you if you withdraw within a specific time period.

Select the best performer of last month (from Seeking Alpha, cnnFn, or one of many ETF/mutual fund sites). Add a contra ETF such as SH to take advantage of a falling market for more aggressive investors. Add sector ETFs to the described four ETFs such as XLY, XLP, XLE, XLF, XLU, IYW, XHB, IYM, OIL and XLU to expand your selection.

ETFs	Money Market	U.S.	International	Bond
Fidelity		Spartan Total Market	Spartan Global Market	Spartan US Bond
Vanguard		Total Stock Market	Total International Market	Total Bond Market
My choice	Fidelity	SPY	Vanguard	Fidelity
Suggest %				

During Market plunge	90%	0%	0%	10%
After plunge	10%	60%	20%	10%

Explanation

- The above are suggestions only. If your broker offers similar ETFs, consider using them.
- Check out any restrictions of the ETFs and commissions.
- 4 ETFs (one actually is a money market fund) are enough for most starters. They are diversified, low-cost and you do not need rebalancing except during a market plunge.
- The percentages are suggestions only. If you are less risk tolerant, allocate more to a money market fund, CD and/or bond ETF.
- Have at least 10% allocated to the money market fund for safety.
- When the market is risky, reduce stock equities (i.e. increase money market and bond allocations).
- The symbols for Fidelity ETFs are FSTMX, FSGDX and FBIDX.
- The symbols for Vanguard ETFs are VTSMX, VGTSX and VBMFX.
- If you are more advanced, use additional sector ETFs to rotate. Also buy long-term bond funds (such as 30-year Treasury) when the interest rate is 10% or more.

#Filler: Glad to be an investor

After watching the following YouTube video, I am glad my parents did not push me to play piano and also glad I do not have any musical gene. How can I compete with this kid?

https://www.youtube.com/watch?v=yf0B4rVoq44

Also glad not into some life-threatening professions such as surgical doctors, soldiers, fire fighters, etc. I can make mistakes in investing from time to time without suffering from the consequences. With the uptrend market for most of the last 50 years, most investors should make good money. Thank God.

4   Simplest way to evaluate stocks

Beginners should trade ETFs only. This chapter is for the readers who are ready or getting ready to trade stocks. In general, ETFs are diversified, less volatile than trading stocks. However, stocks offer higher profit but higher risk.

Many stock researches have already been done recently and some are available free of charge. I have no affiliation with Fidelity except I retired from it. You can open an account with them with no balance. Their Equity Summary Score is one of the best indicators; I check out **value** stocks with scores higher than 8. Concentrate on fundamental metrics such as P/E for long-term holds, and momentum metrics for short-term holds. Add criteria to limit the number of screened stocks. Finviz.com is a free screener.

Several sources

The popular ones are Morningstar, Value Line, The Street and Zacks (currently free for rankings of individual stocks). If they are not free, check out whether they are available from your local library. I have 3 simple ways to evaluate stocks starting with the simplest. In addition, read the articles on the selected stocks from Fidelity, Finviz, Seeking Alpha and many other sources for further evaluation.

Fidelity

Select only stocks that have Fidelity's Equity Summary Score 8 or higher. There is tons of information about a stock. Once in a while I did not agree with this score such as SHOP and ZM that scored high in August, 2020. Include the following for your analysis.

A modified stock selection based on a magazine article

Most metrics are available from Finviz except EV/EBITDA.

1. Forward P/E (expected earnings and not based on the last twelve months). It should range from 5 to 15 (10 to 25 for high tech stocks). EV/EBITDA (from Yahoo!Finance) is a better choice as it includes the debts and cash than P/E; it would be more effective if it uses forward earnings. If you do not use EV/EBITDA,

ensure Debt/Equity is less than 0.5 except for the debt-intensive industries.

2. ROE (Return of Equity) measures how well the company uses the capital. I prefer stocks with ROE greater than 5%.

3. Volatility. Conservative investors should select stocks with a beta of less than one (i.e. less volatile).

4. Insider Transactions for sales (i.e. negative) should be less than 5%. If it is -5%, most likely the insiders are dumping it.

5. Compare the metrics such as P/E and Debt/Equity to its five-year average and its competitors (available in Fidelity).

6. Momentum. Check out the SMA-50 (actually SMA-50%) and SMA-200. Ideally they should be positive. SMA-50% is especially important for stocks you do not want to keep for a long time.

7. Check out articles on the stock as some recent events (for example a new lawsuit) have not been included in the metrics.

8. Compare the trend of the sector this stock is in. Under Finviz, enter the related sector ETF.

Summary
The sources are Fidelity (Equity Summary Score and various comparisons), Finviz and Yahoo!Finance (for EV/EBITDA). Value stocks should be held longer.

Category	Score / Metric	Value /Momentum
Score	Fidelity's Equity Summary Score	Both
Value	EV/EBITDA	Value
	P/E cheaper compared to 5-year avg.	Value
	P/E cheaper compared to its sector.	Value
	Insider Purchases	Both

Safety	Debt/Equity	Value
	Compare it to its sector.	Value
Momentum	50-SMA%	Momentum
	200-SMA% (for long term holds).	Value
Articles	Check out latest events	Both
Market	No purchase if market is risky.	Momentum

A simple scoring system using Finviz

Bring up Finviz.com and then enter the stock symbol.

No.	Metric	Good	Bad	Score
1	Forward P/E[1]	Between 2.5 and 12.5, Score = 2	> 50 or < 0, Score = -1	
2	P/ FCF[1]	< 12, Score = 1	>30 or < 0, Score = -1	
3	P/S[1]	< 0.8, Score = 1	< 0, Score = -1	
4	P/ B[1]	< 1, Score = 1	< 0, Score = -1	
	Compare quarter to quarter of last year			
5	Sales Q/Q	> 15%, Score = 1	< 0, Score = -1	
6	EPS Q/Q	> 20% , Score = 1	< 0, Score = -1	
			Grand Score	
	Stock Symbol Date[2]	Current Price	SPY	

Footnote

[1] Negative values for Sales (due to accounting adjustments), Equity and Book are possible but not likely.

[2] The last row is for your information only. SPY is used to measure whether it will beat the market by comparing the return of this stock to the return of SPY.

The Score

Score each metric and sum up all the scores giving the Grand Score. If the Grand Score is 3, the stock passes this scoring system. Even if it is a 2, it still deserves further analysis if you have time. You may want to add scores from other vendors. To illustrate on using Fidelity, add 1 to the score if Fidelity's Equity Summary score is 8 or higher. Monitor the performance after every 6 months or so to see whether this scoring system beats the market.

Very basic advice for beginners
Beginners should stick with U.S. stocks with Market Cap greater than 800 M (million), Debt/Equity less than .25 (25%) except for debt-intensive industries such as utilities and airlines and Forward P/E between 5 to 20 (25 for high-tech companies). These metrics are all available from Finviz.com, which is free.

Do not have more than 20% of your portfolio in one stock (unless it is an ETF or mutual fund) and do not have more than 30% of your portfolio in one sector.

For more conservative investors, buy non-volatile stocks whose beta (available from Yahoo!Finance) is less than 1. Beta of 1 represents the market (the S&P 500 index). For example, a stock with beta 1.5 statistically fluctuates more than 50% of the market and hence it is very volatile.

Try paper trading to check out your strategy and your skill in trading stocks. If your broker does not provide one, use a spreadsheet to record your trades or check the availability of simulator.investopedia.com.

#Filler: Silence is golden

I am glad I did not give advice to a friend who had to decide whether to take a lump sum payment or an annuity. The correction in March, 2020 would wipe out a lot of his portfolio if he took the lump sum payment. No one would share his profits when the predictions are correct, but the blame if it does not materialize.

It is the same in investing that nothing is certain. With educated guesses, we should have more rights than wrongs especially in the long run.

5   Simplest technical analysis

When the stock, the sector that the stock is in and the market are all above its SMA-N averages (Single Moving Average for the last N sessions), most likely the stock is trending up.

1. Bring up Finviz.com from your browser.

2. Enter SPY. Write down the SMA-200 (Single Moving Average for 200 sessions). Positive numbers indicate that the trend for the market is up.

    However, the market could be peaking or overbought. Be careful when SMA-200 is over 5% and / or RSI(14) is over 65%. RSI is a metric on over bought / under bought.

3. Enter the sector ETF the stock is in. Write down the SMA-50. Positive numbers indicate that trend for the sector is up.

    However, the sector could be peaking or overbought. Be careful when the SMA-200 is over 10% and / or RSI(14) is over 65%.

4. Enter the stock symbol. If your average holding period of the stocks is 200, use SMA-200 and so on. I recommend SMA-200 for holding value stocks long term and SMA-50 for momentum stocks. Write down the SMA-N for your stock. Positive numbers indicate that the trend is up.

    However, the stock could be peaking or overbought. Be careful when the SMA-200 (or SMA-50) is over 25% and / or RSI(14) is over 65%.

If the above three criteria and the fundamental criteria are satisfied, most likely it is a good buy. If you buy sector ETFs or mutual funds only, you can skip step #4. In any case, use stop loss to protect your investment.

6 The best strategy

The best-kept secret in investing is to buy a weighted ETF. I use SPY as an example here. This ETF is well diversified as it keeps all 500 stocks in the S&P 500 index. The ETF has higher position (in percentage) on stocks with higher market cap. The stocks with higher market caps usually grow the market cap by having good management and good products. The bad stocks are deleted from the index periodically.

The second best-kept secret is using simple market timing as described in this book to reduce the losses in market crashes.

It is very hard to beat this strategy. You do not need any knowledge in investing, and you only spend a few minutes every month to time the market. The market is risky when the metrics show you so such as the price is close to the simple moving average in using SMA-350 method; in this case you time the market more frequently.

7 Don'ts for beginners

- Do not use leverage: options, margin and leveraged ETFs.
- Do not short stocks.
- Buy low and sell high.
- Buy value stocks. Sell profitable stocks after a year and losers before holding 12 months for favorable tax treatments in non-retirement accounts. Be a turtle investor.
- Limit momentum trades.
- Use stops to protect your portfolio.
- Do not follow 'experts' blindly (most have their own agenda).
- Do not trade penny stocks (i.e. stocks less than 200 M and/or price less than $1 to my definitions).
- Venture into momentum trading when you have knowledge and time. Avoid trading systems that are available.
- Do not day trade. Most beginners lose most of their money.
- Do not take classes / seminars that promise you big money - if it works, they will give out their secrets.
- Be selective on investing subscriptions.

8   Summary

The following improves the odds of success but there is no guarantee.

Risky Market?

Bring up Finviz.com. Enter SPY. If both SMA-50% and SMA-200% are both negative, do not invest especially when SMA-50% is more negative than SMA-200%.

Evaluate value stocks from others' researches

Gather a list of stocks from screens and/or recommendations from magazines. Use researches that are free. Value stocks should be kept for at least 6 months. In six months or so, evaluate the bought stocks again to see whether you want to sell the stocks. Some other sites may provide free trial or one-time evaluation: IBD, GuruFocus, Zacks and Morningstar. Fidelity requires an account but there is no minimum position.

Name	Pass Grade	Link
Fidelity's Equity Summary Score	>=8	
Value Line[2]	Timeliness > Average	
	Proj. 3-5 yr.% > 5%	
VectorVest[1]	VST > 1 and RV > 1	Link

1   Should be available from your local library.

2   Free for limited number of stocks and free trial.

Evaluate stocks

Bring up Finviz.com and enter the stock symbol.

Metric	Passing Grade
Forward P/E	Between 5 and 20 (25 for tech stocks)
P/FCF	< 15 and ratio is positive
Sales Q/Q	>10
EPS Q/Q	>15

Intangible Analysis

Bring up Finviz, Fidelity, Yahoo!Finance or Seeking Alpha (fewer articles now) and enter the stock symbol. To prevent manipulation, the stocks should have larger cap (> 200 M) and higher daily average volume (> 10,000 shares).

Bonus: Simplest way to detect correction

Corrections are hard to detect, hence beginners can ignore this article for now. When the market dips temporarily, it could be the best time to buy. When the market surges temporarily, it could be the best time to sell. Get a list of value stocks to buy and have cash ready. It works great in a sideways market. However, when the market plunges, do not buy any stocks. A correction could lead to a market crash.

How

Technical indicators may detect whether the market is ripe for temporary dips. On the average, I estimate there are two dips a year, but this number fluctuates widely. If the price is far higher than the SMA, it may be peaking for that period. RSI(14), the relative strength index using the last 14 days, determines whether the stock is overbought. It is not always reliable.

1. Bring up Finviz.com from your browser.
2. Enter SPY (an ETF simulating the S&P 500 index) on "Search Ticket".
3. SMA-200%, Single Moving Average for 200 days, indicates how far away the current stock price is from the SMA-200.
4. The market is peaking when SMA-200 is over 5%.
5. RSI(14) can be located in the right hand side of the metrics. The market is overbought when RSI(14) is over 65%.
6. When the P/E is greater than 25 (the average is 15), the market may be overvalued. Get it from http://www.multpl.com/
7. Suggested Actions:
    1. Do not buy stocks including ETFs when a correction is expected as indicated by these two conditions (#5 and #6).
    2. Do not want to exit the market totally as the market still could head higher.
    3. Sell some stocks that have reached your objectives. Do not sell more than 25% of your portfolio.
    4. Use trailing stops on the remaining stocks you bought. I recommend that you use 5% less than the current prices and 10% for volatile stocks. Adjust the stops accordingly every month.

5. If you trade SPY or other ETFs stocks instead of stocks, skip the following.
6. When the correction materializes and the reverse conditions occur (i.e. 5% is less than the last peak and/or RSI(14) is less than 30%), buy the ETFs and/or the stocks in your buy list.

Go back to step #1.

Bonus: Investing for 'lazy' folks

You have better things to do than investing or you do not have the time, the desire to learn and/or expertise in investing. You should be better off to buy ETFs.

I recommend the following 4 ETFs. If you have $100,000 to invest, buy $25,000 for each recommended ETF. Consult your financial advisor before taking any action. The recommended ETFs should have a large market cap (the ETFs themselves and not the stocks they hold) and have a high volume.

Most returns started on July 1 and ended on July 1 the following year; this article is written on July 20, 2021. All are annualized returns for easy comparison. Fees, commissions and dividends have not been included; you can add the dividend yield and prorate it for YTD return.

Symbol	Name	YTD[1] Return	1 Year[2]	5 Years[3]	Bear[4]
IWF	Russel 1000G	30%	34%	40%	-33%
QQQ	QQQ	30%	46%	42%	-31%
VTI	Vang. Viper Tot	34%	22%	42%	-35%
VUG	Vang. Growth	37%	33%	41%	-32%
Avg.		31%	34%	41%	-33%
SPY[5]		34%	21%	39%	-35%
Beat[6]		**-9%**	**60%**	**6%**	**7%**

[1] The start date is 1/4/2021 and the end date is 7/1/2021.
[2] The start date is 7/1/2020 and the end date is 7/1/2021.
[3] The start date is 7/1/2016 and the end date is 7/1/2021.
[4] The start date is 1/2/2008 and the end date is 4/1/2009. My estimates.
[5] SPY is the ETF for the S&P 500 index. It is used as a yardstick.
[6] = (Avg. − SPY) / SPY. Again it does not include fees, commissions and dividends.

Comments:

- The YTD is the only period that this portfolio does not beat SPY (the market to many). It could mean the market could be changing the favorite from growth stocks to value stocks. However, 31% return is far above the average of the market.
- The one-year return beats the market by 60%.
- The 5-year return beats SPY only by 6%, but the return of 41% is nothing to sneeze at.
- All except Vanguard's Viper Total are ETFs for growth stocks. Hence, I expected it would not beat the market, but it still did by 7%.
- You can time the market using the techniques described in this book as often as you can. When the indicator tells you to exit, you can sell these ETFs and reenter the market when it recovers. Riskier investors can buy contra ETFs such as PSQ and SH instead of holding cash when the market is down.
- At least once in a year review the selection. Use ETFdb.com for information. If you do not have time, it is fine skipping the review. When you switch ETFs, taxes should be considered.
- Most ETFs replace some stocks periodically to ensure better appreciation potential.

#Filler "How to make a 50% return"

https://www.youtube.com/watch?v=eEto5nEkf1Y

#Filler Buffett, the person.
https://www.youtube.com/watch?v=w-eX4sZi-Zs

Bonus: Sample portfolio

It is a suggested sample. You need to tailor it to fit your personal requirements and your risk tolerance. In general, you should have an emergency fund for at least 3 months (6 months preferred). Many of our generation have one or even no layoff. However, I estimate the current generation will have 3 layoffs in their work life. It is due to automation, artificial intelligence, global economy, etc.

The rough estimate of stock holding in distribution between stock and bond is equal to 100 – Your Age. To illustrate in the following three portfolios, I use a 30-year old, and hence he should have 70% in stocks and 30% in bonds (including gold, CDs and cash).

In addition, some sectors are better than others according to the market conditions. The following three portfolios are for regular, todays' market and one during a market crash. I use low-cost ETFs exclusively. ETF is exchange-traded funds. They are traded similar to stocks, but most are more diversified; their fees are usually lower than mutual funds.

ETF	Normal	Today (2/2021)	Crashing[5]
SPY[1]	40%	30%	0%
QQQ[2]	5%	10%	0%
ARKK[2]	5%	0%	0%
VTIAX[3]	20%	5%	0%
LQD[3]	15%	20%	5%
GLD	5%	15%	15%
CD	5%	0%	0%
Cash	5%	20%	60%[6]
SH[4]	0%	0%	5%
PSQ[4]	0%	0%	15%

[1] VOO is a low-fee alternative for SPY.

[2] QQQ has more tech stocks, while ARKK is an actively managed ETF specializing in 'disruptive technologies'. During market crashes, avoid them.

[3] VTIAX is an ETF for global companies. LQD is an ETF for corporate bonds.

[4] SH and PSQ are contra ETF to SPY and QQQ. They are shorting the corresponding index. When the market is recovering, switch them back to SPY and QQQ.

[5] Need to balance the allocations about two times a year as ETFs can grow or shrink. When the market crashes, rebalance it right away. All markets will crash, and the last two (2000 and 2008) have an average loss of about 45%. Refer to the chapter "Simplest marketing timing".

[6] Today's low interest rate does not benefit us for CDs. I would leave the cash not invested and wait for the recovery to move back to stocks.

Of course, everyone's situation is different. If you are conservative, do not buy SH and PSQ. If you are afraid of inflation (especially due to the excessive printing of money), allocate more on GLD, a gold ETF.

Do not listen to financial news. They are used by institutional investors / analysts to manipulate the market. Many times they act the opposite from what they preach. This is the primary reason retail investors do not do better. With the GameStop incident, do not invest in most hedge funds. Buffett has proved the hedge funds with their high fees cannot buy an indexed ETF such as SPY.

The above is my recommendation. In the long run, it should work fine. Consult your financial advisor before taking actions. Most info is from RainIsHere, a Cantonese YouTuber.

#Filler: Simple measures to reduce net security.
Do not click any links from unknown sources. Some seem to be ok but not.
MalwareBytes, for checking viruses, is free for download (they do not pay me).

Personally I use a Chromebook for my financial transactions and a two-factor login for my stock trading.

Section II: How to find growth stocks

1   Buy high and sell higher.

When everyone is looking for stocks with the highest value, there may not be any such stocks available. It seems to contradict with my best strategy but it is not intended to. Fundamentals may not show everything about the company such as a new drug, a new product... The all-time high prices usually show that. Buy the stock when it is over the 50-day simple moving average (50 or 200 days depending on how long you usually hold a stock) via Finviz.com.

Buying fully-priced stocks is dangerous even if it may be profitable. To protect your profits:

• Be extra careful in risky market; I prefer not to buy any stock when the market is risky.

• Set stop loss orders. Recommend 10% (or 15% for volatile stocks) less than the current price. If you set a 5% stop, it would be stopped out by normal fluctuations especially for volatile stocks.

• Use Technical Analysis. When the price drops below the moving average you used, sell it. When RSI (14) is high (over 70), check out the reason as it could be overbought.

If you are not very sure, sell half of it. You will not go broke for taking profits.

As in life, there are no guarantees, but using a proven technique / discipline is far better than trading without one. Paper trading ensures the strategy fits the current market conditions, your personal tolerance and requirements.

2   Four strategies for momentum

We have 3 strategies according to the different holding periods. The screen parameters (i.e. selection criteria) are briefly described here. Adjust them to fit your risk tolerance and requirements. Monitor them from time to time as the market always changes.

Metric	Strategy #1	Strategy #2	Strategy #3
Avg. holding period	< 30 days	60 days	90 days
General			
Market Cap	300 M – 2 B	300 M – 2B	2B – 10B
Avg. volume	>100K	>200K	> 300 K
Analyst Rec[1]	Buy or better	Buy or better	Buy or better
Country	USA	USA	USA
Price	>$5	>$10	>$10
Insider Purchases	Positive	Positive	Positive
Fundamental			
P/E	>0	>0	>0
Forward P/E	>0	>0	>0
Return on Equity		>10%	>10%
EPS Growth next year		>15%	>10%
Technical			
Performance	Week up	Week up	Week up
SMA-20%	> 5%		
SMA-50%	> 0%	>2%	
SMA-200%	>0%	>0%	>0%

[1] I usually do not care about fundamentals for momentum stocks.

In addition, they should be in one of the 3 major exchanges: NYSEX, NASDQA and AMEX (Finviz.com allows you to select one exchange at a time).

In general, Strategy #1 does not care about fundamental. Strategy #2 is a typical sector rotation candidate. Strategy #3 cares more about fundamentals.

I recommend to paper trade your strategy using different selection criteria. When you are comfortable, commit a small amount of cash and increase your portfolio size gradually.

Vendors

Most services charge a fee. However, many free sites provide momentum (same as timing) score. Most have a score (same as rank and grade) for timing. Usually they are based on the momentum of the price. If the price jumps very fast and high, this score is high. Use stops to protect your profits. When the price is below a set price (such as 10% from your purchase price), use a market order to sell it. When the timing score is the highest, be very cautious as it cannot go any higher, or a peak is close.

Example

Here is an example of how to find the momentum stocks for your portfolio.

Bring up Finviz.com. Select Screener. Select 20-Day Simple Moving Average above 20%. Sort the screened stocks with this parameter. Today I have about 100 stocks.

Limit your selection to fit your requirements and preferences. Here are some sample criteria: U.S. companies only, capital cap over 100 M, price over $2 and relative volume over 1. Ignore ETFs.

Check whether the screened stocks are peaking (say they have appreciated over 100%) and/or overbought (RSI(14) > 65). Check the reasons for recent surges and evaluate whether the momentum would continue or not. Check out any insider purchases at prices close to market prices.

Strategy #4

This is a variation of the described three strategies. I explain it with a step-by-step approach in implementing it using Finviz.com. Bring it up by typing Finviz.com in your browser.

1. Only buy momentum stocks when the market is not risky. When the tide is up, all ships will flow up. Check out my market timing technique. In the simplest way, enter SPY (or any ETF that simulates the market) in Finviz.com. If SMA-20%, SMA-50% and SMA-200% are all positive, most likely the market is not risky. 20% is more important than the other two.

2. Screen. The following are my preferred metrics and you can change them to suite your requirements and risk tolerance.

   From Descriptive tab, Select Small (300M to 2B) for Market Cap, Over 100K for Average Volume, Over 2 for Relative Volume, USA for Country and Over $5 for Price. Repeat it for other ranges such as 100M to 4B in the Market Cap. For 100 M market cap, use over $1 for Price; increase the price for larger market cap such as using 'over $2' for 200 M market cap.

3. From Fundamental tab, select Positive in Insider Transaction.

4. From Technical tab, select 10% above SMA-50 in SMA-20 (Simple Moving Average for the last 20 days) and 20% above 200-SMA in SMA-50. If you have too many stocks, reduce the 10% to 8% or less. Change the selection if they are not desirable for you and/or the current market conditions.

   As of 11/07/2016, I have the following 4 stocks: AAOI, BOOT, LC and NILE. They already had good price increases.

5. Click on the selected stocks one by one such as AAOI. From most other metrics, it is not a value stock. The Forward P/E is 16. Hence, it has some value despite the high P/E of 80. All SMA%s are positive which indicate it is trending up.

6. After you bought the stock, use stop loss to limit any losses especially in this risky market. Conservative investors should stay away from risky markets. I would set a 15% stop loss (i.e. sell it via a market order when it loses 15%).

7. Most likely you will not or cannot buy a stock via a discount price when the stock is trending up.

8. Save the screen with a name such as Momentum, so you do not have to reenter the metrics again.

9. Finviz does not provide a historical database. You can run the test every week (or monthly) and write down the results. Only invest with real money when you're comfortable with your tests. If your expected maximum loss is 50%, double your portfolio size as the money you can afford to lose.

10. Making 55% profitable trades could be very profitable.

11. There are many variations and parameters to this strategy such as RSI(14), Double Bottom in Pattern and New High in 52-Week High/Low.

12. If your purchased stock is moving up, review it every month (preferable every week) and set up a trailing stop. To illustrate, when it is up by 20%, set the stop at the current price (not the price you paid for the stock).

#Filler: The Ten Commandments of Investing.

http://www.investopedia.com/articles/basics/07/10commandments.asp

Set goals. * Personal finances in order. * Ask questions. * Do not follow the herd. * Due diligence. * Be humble. * Be patient. * Be moderate. * No unnecessary churning. * Be safe. * Do not follow blindly.

My additions: * Diversify. * Study market timing. * Protect your losses and profits. * Monitor your screens and your metrics. * Be emotionally detached from investments. * Learn from mistakes. * Stay away from bubbles. * Be socially responsible.

3 Common parameters for screening

Different styles of investing use different parameters for screening stocks. Here is my summary/guideline on parameters in using finviz.com. Finviz.com is not complete but it is the best free screener that incorporates both the fundamental and the technical criteria. The first table is for Growth. The next one is for finding larger stocks.

Growth

Growth Screen	Common	Technical	Momentum
General			
Market Cap (M)	>50	> 1,000	>500
Price	>1	>10	>5
Exchanges (Major 3)	In	In	In
Avg. Volume	>50K	>200K	>100K
Fundamental			
Forward P/E	<30	<30	<30
Return of Equity	>5	>0	>0
QQ earning	>10%	>15%	>20%
QQ sales	>5%	> 5%	>10%
PEG	<1	<1	<1
Analyst recs.	Buy or +		
Technical			
Price above 200 SMA	Yes	Yes	
50 SMA	Yes	Yes	Yes
RSI	< 75	< 75	

Short-term trends are important for momentum stocks.

Explanation

The above are suggestions only. Adjust them to your personal preferences and risk tolerance.

- Finviz screener lacks ranges, such as you cannot specify a range of market cap and exchanges. You search the stocks and deselect the stocks that do not fit your requirements.

- Average Volume. When the price of the stock is less than $3, double the average volume requirement. In most cases, 10K is quite acceptable to me. When the volume is small, you may have to pay more (a.k.a. spread) to trade.

- There are many fundamental metrics such as Debt/Equity and Price/Free Cash Flow not included here and they should be included in your further evaluation. Each industry sector has different thresholds. For example, the P/S is very different for a supermarket than a high tech company. Compare the company to the average value of the companies in the same sector. Many sites including GuruFocus.com and Fidelity.com have the average values.

- For momentum stock, you ignore most fundamentals and concentrate on price trend such as SMA-20% and SMA-50%. The higher the percent, the higher away from the average.

- For growth stocks, ensure the PEG (P/E growth), quarter-to-quarter earnings and quarter-to-quarter sales are above the averages in their sectors and/or the market.

- Technical analysis favors large cap stocks with large volumes. I prefer stocks with positive earnings.

- Include 3 basic technical indicators here. I would like to buy stocks when they're above its 200 SMA (Simple Moving Average for the last 200 trade sessions). It is they're in up trend.

- RSI(14) indicates whether the stock is oversold (>60) or under bought (<35). The values are for an average company and they are different for every company and its sector.

- You may want to check out your strategies using a virtual account from your broker or a simulator.

A general guideline for larger stocks

Criteria	Value
Description	
Relative Volume	Over 2 M
Country	USA
Institution Ownership	Over 50%
Technical	
20-Day Simple Moving Avg.	>10%
Volatility	Week – Over 3%
RSI(14)	>40%
Fundamental	
Market Cap	>1B
ROE	>10%

- You may want to vary the parameters. I prefer USA companies. If you use foreign countries, ensure larger companies and/or in countries that has regulator similar to our SEC.
- For value investors, select Forward P/E less than 20 and earning is positive.
- Check out how many analysts following the stock.
- In my example, I find 15 stocks for that time. I narrow them to 2. First, I skip all stocks that already have more than 10% rise recently. They may have risen too high already.
  Select profitable stocks with forward P/E less than 25. "Debt/Equity" is less than .5 (50%). Then, ROI is higher than 25%.

4   Good News/Bad News

This strategy responds to the news. Hence, it is faster and it could complete the trade in a few days or even a day.

If you started on the day Trump announced the tariff and lasted today (4/2018), you should make some good money. You buy SPY (or similar ETF) when there is bad news and sell (and buy contra ETFs for more speculative traders) when there is good news such as China's announcement on negotiating trade retaliation.

You should adjust the strategy to your individual risk tolerance. In any case, use trailing stops to protect losses. To illustrate, buy SPY when it is 1% down and double the bet when it is 2% down.

This strategy will not work when there is a defined trend such as heading to a market crash. As always, practice the strategy not with real money until you're comfortable.

It is simple but most retail investors just do the opposite: Buy High and Sell Low. The flow of money to/from money market funds turns out   to   be   a   reliable   contrary   indicator.

The Early Recovery in 2003 and 2009 and the later part of June, 2012 could be the best time to buy.

The above represents buying at low prices and selling at high prices. Considering P/E (positive 'E' only), buy at low P/E of a stock, a sector and the market (via an ETF) and sell them respectively at high P/E.

Here are some hints when to buy and sell with this strategy:

- Sell when everyone including your silly mother-in-law is making good money and all participants think they're financial geniuses. It could be the riskiest time. The high interest rates (my yardstick is over 5% for Fed Discount rate, the best rate the Fed lends to the banks) usually confirms this as folks falsely expect better returns even though they pay more on interest to borrow money to buy stocks.

- Do not buy the stocks that were the bubble-forming stocks such as the technology stocks in 2001-2002 and the bank stocks in 2008-2009 as some 'optimists' think it is time to return and usually they're wrong.

  Do not think the stock is a good deal when it loses half of its value. Buy them only when the root problem has been fixed. The best time to return to the market after a market plunge is usually two years after the market plunge (2003 for the market plunge in 2000 and 2009 for the market plunge in 2007/2008). Many bubble stocks never recover and many of these stocks take more than 3 years to recover. Their prices appear to be low, but no one can predict the bottom unless it goes to zero.

- Be careful in the sectors or group of stocks that have a winning streak for more than two years. Most likely they will correct. Use a stop loss to protect your profits if you want to keep them.

  You could have saved a lot if you used this strategy on tech stocks in 2000. As of 2015, dividend stocks could be the next sector to burst, but only time can tell. Do not fall in love with a stock. Yesterday's winners could be tomorrow's losers, and vice versa.

  'Buy and hold' has been dead since 2000. We have two market plunges with an average loss of about 45% from their peaks.

- Do not buy dividend stocks solely for their dividends. Most of them are matured companies; most have less growth and hence less appreciation potential. They usually lose less value in a recession after dividends. Income investors are chasing them for higher dividends than bonds.

  Except from Roth accounts, when you withdraw from your retirement accounts, your dividends will be treated as income. Check the current tax rates for income and dividend from taxable accounts.

- Buy value stocks that seem to be bottomed. It is hard to identify the bottom. When the appreciation potential outweighs the risk, it could be a buy.

- No one can predict consistently the market bottom. However, use your better judgment with educated guesses to gain an edge. Refer to the exit point using the 350-day SMA from the chapter on detecting market plunges.

- Buy the stocks that have been losing money but their burn rates can last for the entire recession. They're risky but the potential profits are great. There were many in 2003 and 2009. Even in a bad economy in 2012, a few corporations had historically low P/Es.

- Buy value stocks with a turnaround sign such as when the SMA-50% is positive.

- Buy against the experts who have unconvincing predictions. They usually exaggerate the rosy outlooks of the companies in order to sell the stocks they own. This is one of the few times you should bet against them. Use your better judgment to ensure how false their predications could be.

Using Citicorp (symbol C) as an example

Following the chapter on avoiding bank stocks, buying this stock at $550 a share could be avoided. After the big plunge in 2008, I believe it has long-term profit potential. Accumulate this stock if you believe C will be profitable in 10 years (2024) or so. Do not sell it unless there is potential for a market plunge. If so, buy it back after the plunge. One's opinion.

With our market timing (defending sector may return in two years), I checked it in mid 2009, about 2 years after the start of the market plunge. Optionally I could use the SMA-350 of the stock to determine the reentry point. However, it had no meaning due to the big plunge from $550. On 8/2009, C's P/E was negative, so I did not buy it.

Alternatively buy it for when there is a big drop in P/E regardless of the current price as follows. We started when the P/E is about 40. Normally I buy it when the P/E is at around 20. Take an exception for turnaround stocks.

Date	P/E	Price
06/2010	40	40
01/2011	13	49
08/2011	9	32

The above is for illustration purposes only, so the numbers are not precise.

As of 6/12/2014, I expected a correction, so I sold it at about $48. I only trade this kind of stocks when I see long-term appreciation potential. The other three important metrics are P/B, P/S and RSI(14). Use Forward (same as Expected) P/E if possible. The most important metric for lenders is the quality of the loans, which is hard to evaluate for retail investors. The other factor is any serious, pending lawsuits. When Lehman Brothers was gone, the governments will chase after the institutions that sold the derivatives.
Update 8/2019. C's stock price is $62.

#Filler: Miss Mia

In my first job just after the Vietnam War, every one tried to date my beautiful office mate Mia except me. If we married, then her name would be Mia Pow. She would be very popular, or very unpopular without showing her beautiful face. In any case, when she becomes a mother, she will be Mamma Mia.

BTW. I was the "comfort man" due to the gender gap during the Vietnam War.

5   Different investment styles

There are three major styles to evaluate stocks: Fundamental, Growth and Technical Analysis (TA).

The debate on their benefits could be endless. I believe TA is good for short term (1 month for stocks), growth for intermediate term (say 3 months) and fundamental is good for longer term (say 6 months). Here is my summary of the two (I place Fundamental and Growth into the same group for discussion here).   Market sometimes favors value (i.e. fundamentals) and sometimes growth.

TA depends mostly on the stock price and hence it predicts the trend better; it also can track oversold conditions. TA would catch the stock movement, but not by fundamental or growth metrics.

- TA.
  Most TAers do not care about fundamentals, but price and volume. They do have good arguments. A lot of data about the stock are not available or too late to be effective such as a new drug discovery, being acquired, or a serious lawsuit pending.

  The following are two illustrations on how TAers can benefit.

  When the insiders and/or analysts know about some promising new products or positive unexpected earnings, they buy and tell their families to buy. I do not judge whether it is Illegal insider trading or not. TAers notice the rise of the stock price with increasing volume and they buy. Many times the last ones to buy may end up losing money as the insiders would unload them especially when the stock prices are over-valued.

  When the institutional investors (pension fund managers and fund managers) are buying a specific stock, the stock volume and its price will both rise. TAers would notice them from the charts and jump on the wagon. To me, this is the basic reason on how good day traders make money. It usually takes a week for an institutional investor to finish trading a stock.

- Fundamentals.
  They look at the companies' metrics such as P/E, expected P/E, PEG, debt, sales growth, etc. A good company's stock price with rising profit and rising sales should appreciate in the long term. Some short the stocks of companies with bad fundamentals. In some cases, data is hidden in the financial statements that most metrics do not detect.

To conclude, the best TAers and the best fundamentalists usually make money in either market in the long run. However, fundamental analysis is easier to master and they have made more money than TAers in the long run. You find a lot of successful fundamentalists from Buffett and his followers, but not too many successful TAers. Some successful TAers even lose their accumulated fortunes. Be warned that if you do not know what you're doing in either discipline, you will lose money. Learn it and trade it on paper before committing even small amounts of real money to it.

The best way is use both disciplines in selecting stocks as described below.

- When your chart(s) displays a candidate to buy, take a look at the fundamentals. If the fundamentals are bad, be cautious. Some screens can search for the stocks with good technical patterns (Finviz.com is one).

After you spot a bargain stock to buy via the fundamental metrics, check out its SMA-200 (Simple Moving Average for the last 200 trade sessions) or any duration that fits your purpose. If the price is above the moving average, it could be a buy.

6   Know your stocks and your self

You need to know yourself. Are you a growth investor or value investor? This book is on value stocks. You need to determine your risk tolerance. To reduce risk, you need to diversify such as not having more than 25% of your portfolio on one sector and not 25% on one stock unless your portfolio is small.

They are several ways to find and analyze stocks.

1. Find stocks.
2. Fundamental analysis using others' research. I would like to stick with value stocks and concentrating in growth metrics.
3. Intangible analysis.
4. Qualitative analysis.
5. Technical analysis.
6. Place order.
7. Sell the stock.

Do not buy stocks when the market is risky. Protect your stocks with stops.

The essence of this book

Let the profit rise and at the same time protect your profit.

Use trailing stops. To illustrate with a 10% stop, set the stop at 10% of the current price, not the bought price. You need to change the stop when the price rises but do not change it when the price falls. Review the stop every month.

To illustrate, the stock price rises to 100, set the stop at 90. When the stock price falls to 90, sell it. When the stock price rises to 200, set the stop at 180.

The stop should be set according to how volatile the stock is. Some stocks are more volatile than others. Most charts show the resistance line. This line assumes the stock price should not fall below this line in normal fluctuations. Set the stop at 2% below this line.

7   *Finviz.com screener*

You should use fundamental metrics for fundamental stocks, growth metrics for growth stocks, momentum metrics for momentum stocks, or a combination. Basically you want to keep the fundamental stocks longer so the market would realize their values.

Finviz.com provides a screening function incorporating both fundamental and technical metrics and is one of the best free sites. Bring up Finviz.com in your browser and select screener. You have 4 tabs: Descriptive, Fundamental, Technical and All. It has the following features:

- The criteria specified can be saved but the number is limited.
- The searched stocks can be saved in a portfolio (for paper trading and performance monitoring).
- Technical indicators.
- For an extra fee, you can have a historical database. This would help you to test your strategies. The historical database is quite limited for some technical parameters only.
- Some advanced technical indicators work well especially useful in momentum trading.
- Use technical patterns. My favorites are Head and Shoulder and Double Bottoms (Peaks).
- Combine fundamental metrics and technical metrics to narrow down your selection.
- Combine fundamental metrics and technical metrics to narrow down your selection.
- Add Insider Trans (> 5% for me), Short Squeeze (> 20%), etc. for specific purposes.
- Candlesticks is hard to master. You need to read a book dedicated to it.

http://www.investopedia.com/terms/c/candlestick.asp
https://www.youtube.com/watch?v=FsqoV1aVrUc&list=WL&index=56

Finviz's screener lacks the following features:

- Stocks with prices trending up in the last several weeks (such as increasing X% in the previous week).
- Using exponential moving averages that supposedly have better predictive power than simple moving averages for momentum investing.
- Selecting ranges such as selecting all three major exchanges and market cap ranges.
- P/E for an ETF. It can be obtained from other sources such as ETFdb.com.
- When the earnings (E) is negative, you may have the wrong values for P/E and the metrics using E. For example, if you want stocks with P/E less than 20, the screener returns you stocks with negative earnings.
- Combine fundamental metrics and technical metrics to narrow down your selection.

All of these missing features can be worked around. The paid version may provide better functions.

Links:

Investopedia.
http://www.investopedia.com/university/features-of-Finviz-elite/other-chart-features.asp

How to scan using Finviz (YouTube).
https://www.YouTube.com/watch?v=aQ_0FTg9Cfw
https://www.youtube.com/watch?v=tHtovnCY6uY&list=WL&index=96 (Recommended)

Finviz's screener tutorial.
https://www.youtube.com/watch?v=glMtwB7OVf4&list=WL&index=56

Swing trading
https://www.youtube.com/watch?v=M8sNMhPJINU&list=WL&index=55

Screening using technical indicators (YouTube).
https://www.YouTube.com/watch?v=RZRP2NeSX0s

A screener example

The following is an example. Fine tune the selection criteria according to your personal criteria and risk tolerance.

- Bring up Finviz.com from your browser. Select Screener, the third tab. As of 3/24/2015, we have 7066 stocks.

- For illustration purposes, we would like to find stocks with double bottoms, a positive technical indicator. Select the Technical tab. Select Pattern and then Double Bottom. Now we have 257 stocks.

- Select the Fundamental tab that is next to the Technical tab. Select Forward P/E and then select "under 20". Now, we have 86 stocks.

- Select Debt/Equity less than .5. Now, we have 45 stocks. Some industries such as utilities are traditionally high in debt, so you can use 'less than 1'.

- Select EPS growth Q-to-Q over 10%. Now, we have 19 stocks.

- Select the Description tab. Select Country to USA. Now, we have 17 stocks.

- Select Price > 1. Select Avg. Volume "Over 100K". Select Float Short "Under 10%. Select Analyst Recs. "Buy or better". Now we have 9 stocks.

  Now we can evaluate them one by one using Fundamental Analysis, Intangible Analysis, Qualitative Analysis and Technical Analysis. The purpose of screening is to filter the 7000 stocks to a small number (9 stocks in this case).

Skip the stocks that have the Earnings Date within 2 weeks. If you already have too many stocks in the same industry, skip that stock. You can save the screen when you have registered with Finviz.com. It is free. Check the performance of your selections after 3 months or so.

Other sources

Paper trade and check the actual performance before investing your money. Many popular screens provided by many sites worked before but may not work now. It could be too many folks using the same strategy. Hence it is important to check the current performances of the screen you are using. For yardstick, use SPY or similar ETF that simulates the market. Here are some sources beside Finviz.com.

Your broker

Most broker sites have screen functions. Some have screens to simulate what a specific guru such as what Warren Buffett would buy.

IBD (a subscription service)

From my check on the IBD 50, they're good in the last 10 years, but not that good in the last 5 years – the victim of their own success? They provide stocks from their screens. Most screens are for momentum stocks and large caps. Here are the updated days for specific lists as of this writing.

Stocks Group	Published
Sector Leaders	Daily
Stock spotlight	Daily
Top World	Daily
IBD 50	Mon. and Wed.
Weekly Review	Fri.
Big Cap 20	Tue.

You may want to check out individual stocks with Stock Checkup and then analyze them again. The following are good parameters: Composite Rating, Industry Ranking (finer and better than Sector Ranking) and Relative Price. Understand their parameters and apply accordingly - the same for most other vendors.

IBD prefers large and growing companies with institutional ownership. Some of their parameters may not make sense for small, value and/or turn around companies.

Common parameters

Different styles of investing use different parameters for screening stocks. Here is my suggested parameters in using Finviz.com. Vary them to your risk tolerance and market conditions. Finviz.com is not complete in all functions, but it could the best free screener that incorporates both the fundamental and the technical criteria. The first table is for Value and the next one for Growth. The last one is for finding stocks that the institutional investors are trading.

Screening value stocks

Value Screens	Common	Penny	Micro Cap	Dividend
General				
Market Cap (M)	>500 M	<50 M	50 -200 M	+Mid(>2B)
Price	>5	< 5	1-15	>5
In all 3 Exchanges	In	Not In	Most are In	In
Avg. Volume	>100K	>5K	>10K	>100K
Country	USA	USA	USA	USA
Dividend%				>3%
Float Short	<10%	<10%	<10%	<10%
Analyst Rec	Buy or +	Buy or + if avail.	Buy or +	Buy or +
Fundamental				
Forward P/E	<20	<20	<20	<25
ROE	>10	>10	>5	>15
QQ earning	>0			>0
QQ sales	>0			>0
PEG	<1	<1	<1	<1.2
Payout%				20-50%
P/S	<10	<10	<10	<10
Technical				
Price above 200 SMA	Yes	Yes	Yes	Yes
RSI(14)	< 70	< 70	< 70	< 70

There may be no analysts or very few following penny stocks and micro-cap stocks. QQ is quarter to quarter.

Screening Growth Stocks

Growth Screen	Common	Technical	Momentum
General			
Market Cap (M)	>50	> 1,000	>500
Price	>1	>10	>5
Exchanges (Major 3)	In	In	In
Avg. Volume	>50K	>200K	>100K
Fundamental			
Forward P/E	<30	<30	<30
Return of Equity	>5	>0	>0
QQ earning	>10%	>15%	>20%
QQ sales	>5%	> 5%	>10%
PEG	<1	<1	<1
Analyst recs.	Buy or +		
Technical			
Price above 200 SMA	Yes	Yes	
50 SMA	Yes	Yes	Yes
RSI	< 75	< 75	

Short-term trends are important for momentum stocks.

Explanation

The above are suggestions only. Adjust them to your personal preferences and risk tolerance.

- Finviz screener lacks ranges, such as market cap and multiple of exchanges. Most Finviz's parameters do not have a range option such as Exchanges, so you need to run the screen three times, one for each of the three major exchanges.

- Average Volume. When the price of the stock is less than $3, double the average volume requirement. In most cases, 10K is quite acceptable to me. When the volume is small, you may have to pay more (a.k.a. spread) to trade.

- There are many fundamental metrics such as Debt/Equity and Price/Free Cash Flow that are not included here, but they should be included in your further evaluation. Each industry sector has different thresholds. For example, the P/S is very different for a supermarket rather than a high-tech company. Compare the company to the average value of the companies in the same sector. Many sites including GuruFocus.com and Fidelity.com have the average values displayed.

- For momentum stock, you can ignore most of the fundamentals and concentrate on the price trend such as SMA-20% (Simple Moving Average for the last 20 trade sessions) and SMA-50%. The higher the percent, the higher it is away from its own average. You do not want to hold momentum stocks too long (max. 3 months unless the momentum is still uptrend); personally my max. is 1 month.

- For growth stocks, ensure the PEG (P/E growth), quarter-to-quarter earnings and quarter-to-quarter sales are above the averages in its own sector and/or the market.

- Technical analysis favors large cap stocks with large volumes. I prefer stocks with positive earnings and they are fundamentally sound.

- When the SMA-20%, SMA-50% and SMA-200% are all positive, they should be in an uptrend.

- RSI(14) indicates whether the stock is oversold (>65) or under bought (<30). The range is my suggestion only.

- You may want to check out your strategies using a virtual account from your broker.

A general guideline for Institutional investors

Criteria	Value
Description	
Relative Volume	Over 2 M
Country	USA usually
Institution Ownership	Over 50%
Technical	
SMA-200	>10%
Volatility	Week – Over 3%
RSI(14)	>40%
Fundamental	
Market Cap	>1B
ROE	>10%

- Again, these are my suggested metrics. I prefer USA companies and many are global companies. If you use foreign countries, ensure they are larger companies and/or in countries that have regulations similar to our SEC's.
- For value investors, select Forward P/E less than 20 (25 for high-tech companies) and their Earnings are positive.
- Check out how many analysts are following the stocks that you are interested in.

To illustrate, I find 12 stocks. I narrow them down to 3. First, I skip all stocks that already have had more than 10% rise recently. They may have risen too high already.

Select profitable stocks with forward P/E less than 25. "Debt/Equity" is less than .5 (50%). Then, ROI is higher than 25%. Stop when you have reached the optimal number of stocks (3 for me in this example).

If you find too many stocks, tighten the criteria and vice versa. Save the criteria and the selected stocks in a portfolio for paper trading.

Fidelity

Fidelity offers a strong screen function. The most unique feature is incorporating its Equity Summary Score (used to be Analyst's Opinion) and some outside researches such as Zacks and Ford.

From the main menu, select "News and Research", "Screen and Filter" and then "Start a screen".

The following example selects stocks with the following criteria: Security Price (2 to 250), Market Cap. (300 and above), Equity Summary Score (8 and above), Zacks (Strongest) and Ford (Strongest).

It displays the 10 stocks. Research each stock. Read the News about each stock. You may want to use Finviz.com, Yahoo!Finance and other sources to double check.

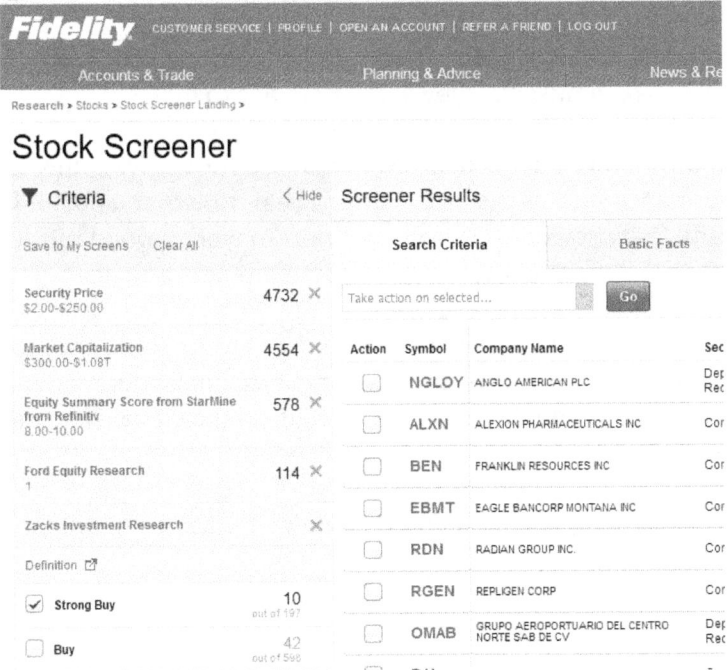

The following describes some of the features.

- Equity Summary Score. It is one of the major metrics I use in my proprietary scoring systems. They are not available to many small stocks. From my limited database in 7/2015 and for short durations, the results are:

Short Term: (7% return for the average)

Metric	Parm. 1	No. of Stocks	%		Parm. 2	No.	%	Predictability
Fidelity Analyst	Buy	150	10%		Sell	279	3%	Good

Long Term: (8% return for the average)

Metric	Parm. 1	No. of Stocks	%		Parm. 2	No.	%	Predictability
Fidelity Analyst	Buy	90	17%		Sell	208	4%	Good

It has its own limits, but they are very minor to me.

First, it does not have a historical database for verifying the screen performance such as the return after a year. However, I do not know any site that provides this function free. To work around this, I save the results in a spread sheet and update the performance.

Secondly, it does not provide many other filter criteria that can be found in other systems such as technical indicators or insider transactions found in Finviz.com. I use other sites for further evaluation.

Most investors should find that this screening is a very good tool and very easy to use.

8   *Fundamental metrics*

ROE

Return of equity (ROE = Net Income / Equity) could be the most important financial indicator to determine how well the management is doing their job. However, in recent years, this metric has been overused and loses its prediction reliability.

The company's return on equity for at least the last five years would indicate how the stock price endures major financial downturns as well as upturns.

Comparing the ROE to the average ROE for the sector is a good indicator on how well the company is managed compared to its peers. Some sectors including utilities have low average ROEs.

Market Cap (Capitalization)

Market Cap = Total no. of outstanding shares * share price

I recommend the beginners buy U.S. stocks with a market cap greater than 800 M (million). Here are the current conventions (everyone's convention is different) and they should be adjusted to inflation.

Class	Market Cap (million)
Nano Cap	< $50M
Micro Cap	$50M to $250M
Small Cap	$250M to $1B (billion)
Mid Cap	$1B to $10B
Large Cap (Blue Chip)	$10B to $50B
Mega Cap	>50B

The higher the cap is, usually the less risky the stock would be. Nano Cap and Micro Cap are reserved for speculators or owners of the companies. Small Cap and Mid Cap are for knowledgeable investors as most institutional investors would skip these stocks in these caps especially Small Cap. Large Cap, Mega Cap and some Mid Cap are the stocks traded by institutional investors. They are thoroughly researched continuously.

My metrics

My current favorites are Forward P/E, PEG, Fidelity's Equity Summary Score, Short % of outstanding shares, Free Cash Flow, ROE and Debt Load / Equity.

In addition, I use many summarized metrics from different sources. For example, one of my subscription services gives me a composite rank for fundamentals and another one for momentum. To illustrate, click here for Blue Chip Growth which is no longer free for stock analysis. Enter IBM as the stock symbol. As of 2/2013, it gives C for a Total Grade, D for Quantity Grade and B for Fundamental Grade. The Total Grade is usually a composite grade of other grades.

Use the metrics to screen through the stocks to reduce the number of stocks for further consideration.

Mid, high and low values of common metrics

Metric	Mid Range	Low Range	High Range
P/E (last 12 months)	< 10	>40	< 4
Price / Cash Flow	< 12	>30	< 4
Price / Sales	< 2.5	>3	< .2
Price / Book	< 2.0	>4	< .2
PEG	< 1.5	>2	< .2

High Range means good values (although in this table it means low numbers), but sometimes it is too good to be true. Low Range means bad values. To illustrate, many internet stocks in 2000 had P/E over 40 (bad) while a neglected bargain stock has a P/E of 3 (supposed to be good). A bargain could also mean they could have some hidden problems. In reality, I prefer the Mid Range. Using P/E to illustrate, it should be between 4 and 10. Adjust the range according to your personal tolerance and the current market conditions. If the market trend is up, you may want to relax the range to 5 to 12 for example otherwise you cannot find too many stocks for further evaluation.

These values are my selections based on data for about 10 years. They are used for predicting the performance of a stock in a year; review the ranges every 6 months in the current market.

The metrics with the high-range and mid-range values offer better predictions for the stock price appreciation. From the above table, the stocks with the low-range values have a better chance than other stocks to lose money in a year or so. Some favorable numbers could be high values instead of low values such as ROE.

However, the range values could change. When the market favors momentum or you do not keep stocks for less than a month or so, the momentum metrics including PEG and price growth could be better predictors. We need to check to see whether the current market favors which metrics: Value or Growth – some websites and subscription services identify the current favorite. In addition, the performance of each metric should be evaluated every 3 to 6 months. In addition, new range values need to be adjusted with the above table.

Fundamental metrics take a longer time (about 6-12 months vs. 1 month for momentum metrics) for the performance to materialize. The metrics in the above table besides PEG are all fundamental metrics. Except for financial stocks, P/B is always worthless.

Examples of searching with high range values

Stocks with low-range values for most metrics (such as 40 in P/E in the above table) could be risky. Hence, select the stocks with the mid-range value (e.g. 10 for P/E). Avoid the low-range values indicated by the metrics.

Here is one example of selecting stocks with high range values of P/E and P/B. Most likely, you will not find too many stocks with these criteria.

$$E > 0 \quad \text{and}$$
$$P/E < 4 \text{ and}$$
$$P/B < .2$$

E is earning per share and we need the company to be profitable.

High range values could indicate something is wrong with the company, e.g. a lawsuit pending. I would consider a P/E of less than 4 is suspicious. However, very small companies are often neglected by the market, so they could be solid companies. Don't forget to do your due diligence and spend more time in thoroughly evaluating the stock and its industry.

The stocks with the low-range values have a greater chance of losing money in the next year or so. That is proven statistically as a group despite some exceptions. AMZN[2] is not a valued stock by its high P/E or its high P/B. However, if the company is investing for the future by building infrastructure and capturing the market share, you may ignore these unfavorable metrics. Personally I prefer fundamentally sound companies today.

Note. P/B is not a good metric for established companies and / or companies with a lot of research such as IBM. Many metric formulae are outdated due to ignoring intellectual properties, patents and market appeals such as brand names.

Example of a search for mid-range values

E > 0 and
P/E < 10 and
P/E > 4

In this case, you only include companies with positive earnings and P/Es within the range from 4 to 10 exclusively. You should find many companies with the mid-range values of P/Es.

Add other filters such as minimum price, market cap and average volume. If you do not find too many stocks, relax your criteria (start with mid-range values in the table), and vice versa to limit the number of stocks. If you usually find stocks with a screen but not today, it usually means that the market is overvalued and that you cannot find many bargain stocks.

Again, it is the first step to narrow down the number of stocks to be analyzed. Your metrics will not cover stocks with special situations. For example, IBM always has had a high Price/Book value for as long as I can remember and therefore it does not mean it should be excluded.

The searches based on fundamental metrics help us to narrow stocks for further evaluation. Occasionally I abandon the scoring system for some stocks under special conditions.

Compare a company's metrics to its sector's averages
This could be the most powerful comparison: Compare Apples to Apples.

You may want to compare the metrics of a company to the averages of that sector. The average of supermarket's P/S is extremely low and hence it has no meaning to compare a supermarket's P/S to most other sectors. Some sectors like utilities need high debt to run a utility company.

However, when the average P/E or other metric of a sector is suddenly lower than its historical average, it could mean that sector is out-of-favor and/or the sector is having a better value.

This following table compares Apple to its sector and a retail sector on a specific date for illustration. All the metrics will change.

Metric	Apple	Computer	Retail
P/E	11	19	24
(5 year average)	16	17	15
PEG	.6	N/A	1.4
Price /Cash Flow	9.4	8.1	9.2
Price /Book	3.3	3.0	3.6
EPS Growth	-6%	-42%	2.6%
(last 5 years)	62%	45%	11%
Operating Margin	20%	15%	8%
ROE	30%	14%	19%
Debt / Equity	2%	7%	88%
Inventory Turnover	76%	53%	4.55x

From the above table, some metrics only make sense for an industrial sector (Computer for Apple). In this case, you may want to compare AAPL to Computer, and not to Retail.

"Debt / Equity" indicates that the retail sector needs to borrow more than the computer sector for example. Of course retail stores has high Inventory Turnover.

Top down approach

First, compare whether the market is risky. Second, select the best sector; there are many sites including Finviz.com to select the best sector. Then compare the fundamental metrics of the major stocks within that sector.

Some metrics do not apply

Using financial institutions as an example, usually P/B is more useful than P/CF. However, the quality of a loan (not a metric here) is more important than all metrics as we found out in 2007. P/S is more important for retails. However, the expected P/E is most important for most other sectors.

When you believe a sector is the currently best (a criterion available in many screeners), select the best stocks in this sector.

Compare metrics to its five-year average

If the company's five-year average of P/E (available from Fidelity and many other sites) is 20 and today it is 10. It is 100% under-valued by this standard. Also, you may want to try other metrics such as debt/equity and compare it to the five-year average.

Growth Metrics

The growth metrics are growth rates of the stock price, sales, earnings, etc. They are useful for growth investors.

Even for value investors, the earnings growth rate is very important, as most stocks with substantial gains have increased their earnings growth first. If the earnings has grown but the price remains the same (i.e. PEG), then the potential for price appreciation will be higher and most likely it will return to the historical average P/E.

Momentum Metrics

Momentum metrics is part of growth. The rates of increase of the stock price, the volume... are the major metrics. Earnings revision is another one especially in earnings announcement seasons (usually 4 times a year).

Fidelity and many subscription services provide a composite rank with name Timely or similar name. The following could be part of this Timely score: SMA-50, Q-Q sales increase and recent price appreciation. In my momentum portfolio, I use these metrics and ignore all the other metrics as my average holding period is less than 30 days for momentum strategies.

Insiders' buying

Insiders sell their stocks for many reasons. When insiders buy a lot of their companies' stocks at market prices, take notice. Insiders know better than anyone about the health of their companies and their industries.

Select Insiders' purchases from one of the available sites such as Finviz.com. Ignore the option exercises. I prefer the high ratios of Net Total Purchase Value / Market Cap and the purchases by more than one insider. Be careful that the insiders purchase the stocks after selling a similar amount of stock in a brief time span.

OpenInsider is a good site for this info.
InsiderSights is a good one too with more capable tools that would take more time to learn.

Where to get the metrics
You can get this information from the website with no or low cost such as Finviz.com, your broker's site, AAII (very low cost) and Fidelity.

The following subscriptions are at a little higher cost but they are still less than $1,000 per year: Value Line, IBD, Zacks, VectorVest and Stock Screen 123. Many data from different vendors are duplicated such as P/E. You will save time by concentrating on one or two sources.

Many vendors provide a composite metric such as a value metric to cover P/E, debt... and a timing metric to cover Technical Analysis indicators, PEG, price appreciation rate...

Short % is a useful metric available in Finviz.com. For Fidelity customers, you can click on Research and then Stock. Enter the stock name, and then click on Detailed. I find Fidelity's Analysts' Opinions quite useful.

Finviz.com provides a lot of useful information free of charge. It also provides a screen function. The 'Help' button describes Finviz's functions and all the metrics monitored.

Other sources are: Insider Cow, NASDAQ Guru Analysis ...

Monitor the recent performance of the metrics
The predictability of most metrics has proven not to perform consistently as many investors and fund managers found out. My theory is that the specific metric works better in some market conditions than others. To test which ones work better currently, check their performance in the last three months and use those that perform well. This is what my scoring system in the book Scoring Stocks is based on.

Why some metrics fail sometimes
Most investors are using metrics to screen stocks, but few are successful consistently. Some investment companies have top analysts dedicated to projects looking for the right strategy. My guesses why they fail are:

1. Metrics need to be monitored to see its effectiveness on current market conditions.

2. Besides fundamental metrics, there are many intangibles.

3. When they have too many followers on the same metrics, they will not work such as ROE in the last several years.

4. Fundamentals need time (at least 6 months) to reflect the value of the stock. You're swimming against the tide as a fundamentalist. Trading momentum stocks using basic fundamentals will not work.

5. Watch out 'Garbage in and garbage out'. Some emerging countries do not have an organization similar to SEC to ensure the integrity of the financial statements of a company and some audit firms are being paid to cover their eyes. Even though there are frauds in some U.S. companies and with their auditors.

6. The metrics may be derived from obsolete financial statements. Check out the date. The most updated one could be available from the company's website.

7. Some companies borrow a lot of money to dress up the metrics such as P/E and ROE. They will look good short-term but not long-term. Ensure the debt/equity has not been increased recently for this purpose. I recall one utility spin-off had incredible fundamentals except the debt load. It is so high that all these fundamentals will deteriorate in the future due to servicing its high debts.

Footnote

[1] The stocks are classified into sector and then sectors are divided into industries (same as sub sectors). For example, oil is a sector and oil exploration and oil services are industries under the oil sector. For simplicity, I intermix the terms here as many sectors do not need further sub classifications for this discussion.

[2] AMZN is not a value stock by any standard. As of 1/1/2013, its P/E (from last 12 months) is 157 and P/B is 15. Both fall far into my low-range values. Its price rises from 256 from 1/1/13 to 270 today (1/22/13). Today its P/E is ridiculously over 3,000. The investors are betting AMZN's internet sales will take over the concrete stores and its investors do not care about profit but rather for market share. Does it sound familiar in the internet era? Its price momentum is indicated positively by any chart. It may be a good stock for traders, but it is too risky for a swing trader and a long-term investor like me (yes, I wear two hats). I do not short stocks in a rising market, but this could be an exception.

Afterthoughts

- The only recommendation from a very popular investment book I read is to select stocks by the return of equity (ROE). I will save you the time and money to read that book. I read the entire book in an hour at Barnes and Noble's and it saved me some money / time, not to mention cutting down trees for that book. Basically it does not work today.
- DAL has an interesting Debt / Equity of over -1000% due to the negative equity. For a comparison, you may want to use Debt / ABS(Equity).

- Once in a while, I found the financial data was not consistent from different sources. Try to check out any discrepancy in the dates of the financial data of your sources. The financial statements from the company websites usually have the most updated data.

- Current Ratio = Current Asset / Current Liability. If it is below 1, then the company is having a tough time in meeting its current cash obligations.

- Dividend Yield is a valid metric for matured companies. I do not use it to evaluate growth companies or companies that need to plow back cash for research and development.

- If you use Finviz.com, you find three margins: profit, gross and operating. I prefer to use profit margin that is more useful for most companies. The other two may be relevant in some sectors.

  http://www.investopedia.com/terms/p/profitmargin.asp
  http://www.investopedia.com/terms/g/grossmargin.asp
  http://www.investopedia.com/terms/o/operatingmargin.asp

  Use Wikipedia for more description.

- Enron had millions in profits but negative cash flows. Earnings can be manipulated but not the cash flows.

  Insiders' selling usually does not cause any alarm unless excessively. Most insiders sell most of the stocks they have before these companies go bankrupt. Just common sense!

- <u>Why</u> fundamentals are important.
  (http://seekingalpha.com/article/1612442-its-shorting-season)

  On the same day when this article was published, RVLT was up 10% due to increasing sales in the earnings conference. However, the company is still not profitable. It shows how tough shorting is even with good arguments. That's why do not expect every purchase is profitable. However, with the educated guesses, you should beat the market in the long run.

- Due to my ignorance, limited time or my short period of holding stocks, I have not used <u>intrinsic value</u> that often.

  Book value is different from intrinsic value. Book value is calculated by summing up the values of all pieces of a company such as a building and all equipment.

  Intrinsic value is the real value of a company. When two companies have the same book value and market cap, the company that generates more profit than the other one usually has a higher intrinsic value. When the intrinsic value is higher than the stock price, it is underpriced in theory.

  The following <u>link</u> provides more info on intrinsic value.
  http://en.wikipedia.org/wiki/Intrinsic_value_%28finance%29

9   Finviz's parameters

Most metrics are described in Finviz (via Help), Investopedia and/or Wikipedia and my chapters on P/E and fundamental metrics if available. We use the metrics for screening stocks and then evaluating the screened stocks.

The following are my personal comments and why I feel some metrics are more important than the others. Personally I divide the metrics into fundamentals and technical, which are more important for long-term investors and short-term investors respectively.

Compare the ratios to the companies in the same sector (industry) and also its averages from the last few years (5 preferable) from many other websites such as Fidelity.

From your browser, enter Finviz.com. Enter a symbol (I used ABEO for discussion). A chart is displayed with the prices and volumes for the last eleven months. SMAs (Single Moving Average) are displayed sometimes with other technical indicators. Intraday, Daily and Weekly options are available for day traders, short-term traders and long-term traders respectively.

Besides the chart and the metrics described next, it describes what the company does, analysts' recommendations (I prefer Fidelity's Equity Summary), insiders' trading and articles that are good for intangible and qualitative analysis. Many free websites such as Yahoo!Finance may provide a list of articles about the company.

"Financial Highlights and Statements" are materials for more in-depth analysis and they were more important decades ago when most financial ratios had not been calculated for you. It is important for investors with good knowledge in financial accounting. The current version also includes basic financial statements and cash flow for the current (TTM) and the last two years.

A section on Insider Trading is also included. Do not be alarmed when insiders dump small quantities of the stocks. Buying large quantities (e.g. insider transaction more than 5%) at prices close to the market price could be favorable news.

The following metrics are roughly based on the flow of Finviz from top to bottom and left to right. I skip those metrics that I believe are not too important. You can also place your cursor on the metric to retrieve the description from Finviz. Some metrics are left blank to indicate they are not applicable (zero, negative or not available). For example, the Debt/Equity of YRCW in 1/2019 is blank (same as null) due to its negative Equity. From Yahoo!Finance at the time of writing, it has a total debt of 888M.

- **Index**. Most of us trade stocks in the three major exchanges in the USA. Stocks listed over-the-counter are too risky for most of us. Skip the stocks in local exchanges and foreign exchanges unless you are an expert on these stocks and/or have insightful (not insider) information. I screen the stocks and then ignore the stocks that are not in the Dow, NASDAQ and Amex. Other screeners may let you select a group of exchanges.

- **Market Cap** (MC). To me, stocks below 50M are risky even though they could be very profitable. Ensure the Avg. Volume is at least 10,000 shares and / or your order is less than 1% of the average volume. Some small stocks are controlled by the owners and have small volumes. In this case you cannot sell your stock easily.

  Float = Outstanding shares – Insider shares.

  Usually Float does not matter as they are typically the same. However, it does for small companies with large insider shares. Most of these owners do not want to sell their family businesses and hence they reduce the chance of being acquired entirely or partially for good prices. In this case, you may have to hold this stock for a long time or you sell it at a very unfavorable price.

- If **Forward P/E** (a.k.a. Expected P/E) is not provided, use the P/E which is based on the trailing last 12 months (TTM). Alternatively, calculate the E by using the E from P/E and multiplying it by its growth rate. It may not be seasonally adjusted. I prefer using Forward P/E as it provides a better predictability power to me.

Finviz.com leaves the P/E blank (same as null) if the earnings are negative. In this case, I would check out Yahoo!Finance's EV / EBITDA, which also considers taxes, cash and interests. The blank condition is similar to some metrics such as when the asset is negative (they seldom occur).

Earnings Yield is equal to E/P. I call it True Earnings Yield for EBITDA / EV. It is easier to understand. Compare Earnings Yield or True Yield to the annual dividend yield of a 10-year Treasury – with the low interest rate in 2021, skip the comparison.

E/P is easier in screening and sorting the screened stocks. If you use P/E instead of E/P, you need to screen or sort stocks with a clause "P/E > 0".

When the P/E is less than 5, be careful and there may be a reason why it is so low. Many bankrupting companies have low P/Es at one time.

Compare the P/E or Forward P/E with the average P/E for the sector and its average P/E for the last 5 years that are available from Fidelity.com. Some sectors have high P/Es. If the sector is cyclical, the earnings could be affected.

When the prospect of the company is good such as Tesla in 2020, ignore P/E.

- **Cash / share**. It is used to calculate Pow P/E and Pow EY when EV/EBITDA for the stock is not available. To illustrate, if the stock is $10 and it has $10 cash / share without debt (i.e. Debt/Equity = 0), most likely it is underpriced as you can get the whole company for nothing. You should find out why the price is so low. It could be the market ignoring the stock, or there is a serious event happening such as a major lawsuit.

- **Dividend %** is useful for income investors. The payout ratio should not be more than 30% except for matured companies. Most developing companies plough back the profits into research and development, and hence they do not pay dividends.

- **Recs**. Select stocks with 1 or 2. Do not base your stock selection on this recommendation alone. There have been many bad recommendations that could cost you a fortune in losses. Use Fidelity's Equity Summary Score instead.

- **PEG** is a measure of the growth of P/E and hence a growth metric. It is similar to P/E, but it takes the expected earnings growth rate into account. The lower value is better as long as earnings are positive. If earnings are negative, then the reverse is true. It is a defect in using P/E and PEG and that's why I recommend EY (Earnings Yield) and EYG, earnings yield growth.

  If there are two companies with the same P/E, the one with a better PEG ratio is better. If two companies have the same E/P, the company with higher Earnings Growth (EPS Q/Q) would be better for similar logic.

- **P/B**. Book value (= Total Assets – Total Liabilities) may not include intangible assets such as patents. Do not trust it 100%, so is ROE which is based on the book value. Negative equity is possible when Total Liabilities is more than Total Assets. This popular metric is outdated for most matured companies as it is now made up of more intangible assets including patents, management, the quality of their employees, brand names, market share, partners, free cash flow and customer base.

- **P/S**. If two companies are unprofitable, this ratio can be used. A retail company such as Walmart is very different from a research company. This metric is only meaningful for stocks within the same sector or specific sectors.

- **P/FCF**. I prefer it to be greater than 0 and less than 50 for value investors. Most metrics can be manipulated easily, but not this one.

- **Sales Q/Q** reduces the seasonal deviation. To illustrate, retail sales for the Christmas season should be compared to the same season in the prior year.

- **EPS Q/Q**. Same as above. I prefer the growth of EPS over Sales. Both of these Q/Q ratios are growth metrics. When a company terminates its unprofitable product(s), its Sales Q/Q could be down but its EPS Q/Q could be up. In 2000, many internet companies had great Sales Q/Qs but negative EPS Q/Qs.

Q/Q comparison (quarter to quarter) takes out the seasonal variations as Sales Q/Q. I prefer both Sales Q/Q and EPS Q/Q increase. When EPS Q/Q increases far higher than Sales Q/Q, it could mean the EPS Q/Q could be temporary such as the oil company when the oil price rockets.

When the company buys its own shares, EPS could be misleading as E is fixed and the number of shares is reduced. In most cases, the fundamentals of the company have not changed.

- Positive **Insider** Transactions are favorable. Sometimes, they are misleading. Need to scroll to the end of the screen and check out more info there. If the transactions are outdated such as 3 months or so ago, and or they are purchases in a similar amount than the sales a while ago, they are not important. Insiders know the company better than us. So is Institutional Transactions as institutional investors move the market.

- Insider Own, Shares Outstanding and Shares **Float** determine the number of shares that are available for trading. A small Float with a high Insider Own limits trading and the stock should be avoided in most cases. Compare your trade position for the stock to the Avg. Volume.

- **Profit Margin**. I prefer it over Gross Margin and Oper. Margin which does not include interest expenses and taxes. When you sell software, the Gross Margin is high as it does not include development, support and marketing, etc. A retail store has low Gross Margin. It all depends on the industry, and hence it is better to compare companies in the same industry.

- **Short Float**. I prefer it to be less than 10%. If it is greater than 10%, the shorters could find something wrong with the company. If it is over 25% (indicating a possible short squeeze), I would check the fundamentals. If they are good, I would buy expecting a short squeeze potential. It is risky but it has been proven to be profitable for me.

- Technical metrics: SMA-20, SMA-50 and SMA-200. Finviz expresses them in convenient percentages. If they are all positive, it means the trend is up. SMA-20 and SMA-50 are a short-term trend and SMA-200 is a long-term trend. If you are a short-term swing investor, stick with the short-term trend and vice versa. The first two are also used as momentum grades. Many long-term investors do not buy stocks when the SMA-200% is negative.

- **RSI(14)**. If it is greater than 65%, it is overbought. If it is under 30%, it is under-bought for me. Some use 5% up or down than mine. Use it as a reference. Most stocks making new heights are always overbought, and many of these stocks keep on rising. I recommend using trailing stops to protect your profit.

- **Beta**. A volatile stock fluctuates a lot. It is good for short-term traders. A beta of 1 means the stock would fluctuate with the market, and be volatile if it is higher than 1. For volatile stocks (higher than 1), the stops should be higher. For example, if your stops are normally 15%, you may want to use 20% or even higher.

- Management performance is measured by <u>ROE</u>. It is also judged by **Analysts' Rec.** and Institutional Ownership (except for small companies). The confidence of their own ability, the company and its sector is measured by Insider Ownership and Insider Purchases.

  ROE = Net Income / Average Shareholder's Equity
  According to Investopedia, a normal ROE for utilities should be 10% while high tech companies should be 15%. Compare this ratio and many other ratios with its peers that are available from Fidelity.

- Avoid all companies that are going to bankrupt at all costs. Debt/Equity, P/FCF, Cash/Sh., P/B, Profit Margin, Forward P/E, Short Float, RSI(14), SMA20% and SMA50 would give us hints. Need to summarize all the info and study many other factors such as obsoleting products (including drugs).

- Unless you have concrete information, do not buy stocks a week or so before the Earnings Date. It is seldom to make great profits when the announcement is better than the expected.

More useful information:

- The price chart. It has a lot of features such as the resistance line. Some charts include technical indicators such as double top (a bearish warning) and double bottom (a bullish sign).
- Description under the symbol. It briefly describes what the company (sector and industry) does and its country of registration. You want to buy a stock within a sector that is trending up. For example, according to Finviz Apple is in the Consumer Goods sector and the Electronic Equipment industry.

  If you do not want to buy foreign stocks, skip it if it is not listed in the US exchange.
- Articles on the company for qualitative analysis.
- Insider trading. Pay more attention to the insider purchases at market prices. Use common sense.
- The last line lets you open Yahoo!Finance and other sites.

Other important sites

Yahoo!Finance.

From Statistics, you can find Enterprise Value / EBITDA. I call it True Yield when I flip them to EBITDA / Enterprise Value.

In case it is not available, I use Earnings Yield. In my spreadsheet without considering the cell designations,

=IF (Earnings Yield = "", True Yield, Earnings Yield)

Fidelity

Compare the P/E of the average PE of the last 5 years. In my spreadsheet for demonstration,

Cheaper By Historically =IF(PE="","",(Avg. of 5-year PE -PE)/Avg. of 5-year PE)

Compare the P/E of companies in the same sector. In my spreadsheet for demonstration,

Cheaper By To the peers =IF(PE="","",(Industry PE - PE)/Industry PE)

Your broker's website

Your broker website should have plenty of tools to analyze stocks. As of Dec., 2018, Fidelity lets you use their extensive research free by opening an account with no position restriction. I describe some of their metrics that should be beneficial to your research.

- Equity Summary Score. Potentially good buy when it is 7 (8 for conservative investors) or higher. With some exceptions, you should avoid or short stocks if the score is 3 or below. The stocks ranking from 4 to 6 could be turnaround candidates if they are supported by good Q/Q Earnings and/or good news.

- The 5-year averages are good yardsticks. For example, in Dec., 2018, C's P/E is about 9 and the average is 14. Hence it is a value buy.

Other sources

If you have other sources (most require a subscription or being a customer), skip the stocks that have one of the failing grades. The exceptions are a new positive development and increased insider purchases.

Vendor	Grade	Fail
Fidelity	Equity Summary Score	< 7
IBD	Composite grade	< 50
Value Line	Proj. 3-5 yr. return. Also its composite rating	< 3%
Zacks	Rank	5
VectorVest	VST	< 0.7

You may be able to find Value Line and IBD in your library. Try out the free stock reports from your broker first. Finviz and Seeking Alpha should have articles (now fewer free articles from Seeking Alpha) on stocks and earnings conferences, which could have important information after separating from the "welcome" and garbage talks.

Yahoo!Finance has good info. "EV/EBITDA" is better than "P/E" as it considers debts and cash. Most use Earnings from last 12 months, which has poorer predictability than Forward Earnings to me.

When negative values such as Equity in Finviz.com, we need to adjust many related metrics or do not use them at all.

MarketWatch.com has many articles on the market in general and personal investing.

If the stock is close to the Earnings Date (found in Finviz.com), you should avoid trading the stock; as earnings could have a big swing for the stock price. Consult Zacks' ranking which is currently free for individual stocks.

Gurus

It is nice to know how gurus would rate the interested stocks. GuruFocus is a good source. NASDAQ is a simplified version, but it is currently free. Bring up Nasdaq.com from your browser. Select "Investing" and then "Guru Screeners". On the third selection, enter the stock symbol such as THO. Click "Go". You will find how 10 or so gurus would evaluate this stock in theory. Click "Detailed Analysis" for each guru.

Quick and dirty

Many times we need to evaluate a stock fast such as taking action due to some development. Refer to my other article "Simplest way to evaluate stocks". The following should take a few minutes. Bring up Finviz.com and enter the stock symbol.

Using SWKS on 6/10/16 to illustrate, Forward P/E is about 11 (fine between 3 and 25), Debt/Eq. is 0 (fine less than .5), ROE is 30% (fine greater than 5%) and P/PCF is 31 (fine if not negative).

Also, check out Market Cap, Avg. Volume, Dividend, Short Float (fine between 0% and 10%), Country and Industry. Judging from the above, it is a buy.

If you have more time, check out the following: Recom. (Ok if less than 2.5), P/B (fine between .5 and 4), Sales Q/Q (fine if not negative), EPS Q/Q (fine if not negative), Cash/Sh (compare it to Debt/Sh) and Profit Margin (fine >5%). Check some articles described for this stock.

5-minute stock evaluation

It takes even less time than the above "Quick and Dirty". However, I recommend you should spend more time researching stocks.

- From Finviz.com, enter the stock or ETF symbol. Look at the number of reds in metrics. If there are more than greens, most likely it is not a good stock.

- It should be fine if Fidelity's Equity Summary Score is greater than 8.

If you have more time, I recommend you to check the following:

- Check out Forward P/E (E>0 and P/E < 20), Debut / Equity (< 50%) and P/FCF (not in red color).

   - If time is allowed, replace Forward P/E with True P/E (same as "EV/EBITDA"), which is available from Yahoo!Finance and other sources.

- SMA20 (or SMA50 for longer holding period). If SMA20 is > 10%, it is trending up.

- It is fine if the Insider Transaction is positive.
- Be cautious on foreign stocks and low-volume stocks.
- If most of the above are positive, it is likely a buy. As in life, nothing is 100% certain.

Links
PEG: http://en.wikipedia.org/wiki/PEG_ratio
Short %:
http://www.investopedia.com/university/shortselling/shortselling1.asp#axzz2LNDvpemo
Openinsider: http://www.openinsider.com/
Finviz: http://Finviz.com/
terms: http://www.Finviz.com/help/screener.ashx
Insider Cow: http://www.insidercow.com/
Current Ratio: http://en.wikipedia.org/wiki/Current_ratio
How to find quality stocks.

http://seekingalpha.com/article/2381395-how-to-identify-quality-stocks-and-is-there-really-alpha-to-be-had

10   Intangibles

I give a score for each stock I evaluate. Occasionally some stocks with poor scores have great returns and vice versa. In general, the scoring system works. It has been proven statistically and repeatedly from my limited data.
I stick with high-score stocks with some exceptions.

Once in a while I change my scoring system to adept to the current market conditions. To illustrate, the market bottom phase and early recovery phase of the market cycle favor value more than momentum/growth. Here are some of my recent experiences and strategies:

- I double or even triple my stake on stocks with high scores. In the longer term, they are consistently better winners than the average with some minor exceptions. Besides the score, look at the intangibles described in this article.

- Watch out for the stocks with outrageous metrics such as P/E of 4 or less. It could be a big lawsuit pending, an expiration of some important drugs, etc. Also, be careful with scores in the top 5%. From my statistics they do worse than the average. Their problems may not show up in the current financial statements.

- The technology of a tech company cannot be ignored even though the company's P/E is high, that I set a limit of 25 instead of 20 for other stocks. The value of the company's technology and patents will not be shown in the fundamental metrics except from the insiders' purchases at market prices.

  For example, IDCC rose about 40% in 2 days. There was a rumor that Google was buying the company and/or Apple was bidding on it too for its mobile technology. Charts usually would flag this kind of event. For non-charters, use the SMA-20% from Finviz.com. They could be a little late as the charts depend on rising prices.

- There are more acquisitions during a market bottom (same as early recovery). The companies with good technologies are bargains and the larger companies especially those in the same sector understand their values better than most of us. These potentially profitable companies will not be shown by their scores explicitly. When corporations have a lot of cash or the credit is cheap, they are looking for smaller companies to acquire or invest in. The candidates are usually small, beaten up, low-priced and having valuable intangible assets such as technologies, customer base and/or market share of the industry segment. 2009-2012 was just the perfect environment and the before that was 2003. I had at least one stock in each of these periods and they appreciated a lot.

- The opposite is Netflix, Chipotle in 1/2012 and Amazon in 1/2013. They are over-priced by any measure. However, the mentioned companies are investing in the future. The shorters (not for beginners) are having a tough time in making money on them. When their P/Es are higher than 40, watch out. Some could be OK in the mentioned companies, but usually they are not. Do not follow the herd and your due diligence will verify whether they will still go up.

  Use reward/risk ratio. It is based on experiences. To illustrate, if the company has the equal chance to go up 50% and go down 25%, then it is a buy and the reverse is a sell.

- The retail investor just cannot possibly know about some events until they actually happen. For example, ATSC dropped 15% due to losing its second primary customer. Fundamentals cannot predict this kind of events. Charts can signal this event, but usually they are too late unless you watch the chart all day long.

- After a quick run up, TZOO plunged due to missing some negligible earning expectations. It seems the original climbing prices already had the perfect earnings growth built-in.

  I do not understand why a company loses 10% of its market cap when it missed by 1% of the expected earnings. It could be driven up and down by the institutional investors. Evaluate the stock before you act. Acting opposite to the institutional investors could be very profitable for the right stocks. Avoid trading before the earnings announcement dates (about 4 times a year for most stocks).

- The following are not easily found in financial statements: industry outlook, patents, good will, market share, competition, product margins, management quality, lawsuits pending, potential acquisition, pension obligations, advertising icons, etc. That is why we need to read articles on the stocks in our buy list or our purchased stocks.

- The financial data could be fraudulent or manipulated. I do not trust small companies in emerging markets. I have been burned too many times. Check the company names such as foreign names, ADR and their headquarter addresses (from the company profile in most investing sites).

  Earnings can be manipulated with many accounting tricks. A jump in earnings from last year may not be as rosy as it looks. Check the footnotes in the accounting statements. I usually skip financial statements unless I have big purchases in mind as my time in investing is limited.

- Cash flow cannot be easily manipulated. It is good information whether the company will survive or not, but to me it does not prove to be a consistent predictor in my tests, but an important red flag for companies on their way to bankruptcy. Examples abound.

- Repeated one-time, non-recurring and extraordinary charges are red flags.

- Stay away from the companies where the CEOs are over-compensated. As of 7- 2013, Activision's CEO raised his salary by more than 600%, while the stock lost its value in double digits.

- Value stocks. Need to know why they become value stocks (i.e. fewer investors want to own) even they are financially sound. For example, there are two primary reasons for the downfall of a supplier to Apple: 1. Apple is declining in sales and 2. Apple is switching suppliers to replace their product. Technology companies are continually building better mouse traps. They could turn around in a year or so with better products.

Conclusion

Buying a stock is an educated guess that its stock price will rise. Fundamentals do not always work, but they work most of the time:

1. When we buy a value stock, we're swimming against the tide. Hence, we need to wait longer (usually more than 6 months) for the market to realize its value. The exception is the Early Recovery phase (see the Market Cycle chapter) and it has faster and larger returns than most other stocks from most other stages of the market cycle.

2. Some metrics are misleading. Book value could be misleading for an established company such as IBM. The image of the cowboy in a tobacco company could be a very important asset that is not included in its financial statement.

3. The market is not always rational.

Afterthoughts

- Brand names of big companies are one of the most important intangibles. Here is a strategy to buy big companies in a down market. It has been proven that it works. However, do not just buy these companies without analysis.
  http://seekingalpha.com/article/1324041-buying-brand-names-in-a-bear-market-can-make-you-rich

- The reputation of a company takes a long time to build but a bad incidence to destroy in the case of GM such as the delay in recalling the killer switches.

11   Qualitative analysis

This is the last analysis to evaluate a stock fundamentally. Then the next is technical analysis which is used to find an entry point (also the exit point) for the stock.

Where quantitative analysis fails and why

I find that some stocks with high scores fail and some stocks with low scores succeed as indicated by my performance monitor. The scoring system still works statistically for the majority of my stocks.

- Reasons why stocks with low scores perform in addition to the described in the last discussion:

  o Over-sold. The institutional investors (fund managers and pension managers) dump them first, and then followed by the retail investors. These big boys will buy these stocks back when they reach a certain price range. RSI(14), a technical indicator described in the Technical Analysis article, is useful to detect these over-sold stocks. This metric is readily available from many sites including Finviz.

  o The falling price (P) improves all fundamental metrics that have the stock price such as P/E and P/Sales. However, the trend of the price is down.

  o The company has turned around after fixing its problems and/or the market has changed for the better.

  o The current problems have been resolved but not known to the public. It includes resolving a lawsuit, a new product, a new drug, or a new big order, etc.

  o Heavy purchases by insiders. The company's outlook is not shown in its financial statements. Sometimes the insiders hide them so they can buy more of their companies' stocks for themselves.

- Reasons why stocks with high scores plunge in addition to the described in the previous discussion:

  o The company's fundamentals and its prices have reached or closed to the maximum heights. They have no way to go but down. It is particularly true when the stock's timing rating is at or close to the highest point. TTWO that I gifted to my grandchildren had been 5-baggers in the last few years before it plunged in 2018.

  o It has reached its potential value (or a target price) and it is time for many investors to take profits.

  o Sector (or stock) rotation, particularly by institutional investors who drive the market.

  o The outlook of the company, its sector and/or the market is deteriorating.

  o The stock price may be manipulated. There are many reasons to pump and dump the stock. Shorting is not recommended for most investors. However, some experienced shorters make money consistently when they find valid reasons to short stocks.

  o It could be due to a new serious lawsuit, a new competing product or drug, canceling a major order, etc.

  o Downgrade by analysts. They could spot some bad events such as product defects, violations of regulations or accounting errors / frauds. The downgrades are more important than the upgrades that could have conflict of interest.

  o The financial statement had been manipulated. The SEC may ask for an investigation.

  o Does not meet the consensus in earnings announcements, which have been over-acted by many investors.

Qualitative Analysis

We need to do further analysis after the quantitative analysis and the intangible analysis. Check out the company's prospects. Check out the date of the article and any potential hidden agenda items from the author. Older articles may not have much value.

Be careful on 'pump-and-dump' manipulation written by authors with a hidden agenda. It has happened especially on small companies before even SeekingAlpha.com has its share. Here was an article that tells you to sell NHTC. There was another article to tell you to buy ARTX. They fit into this category.

The sources are:

1. Seeking Alpha.
    Type the symbol of the company to read as many articles on the company as you have time for. Today this site and many other similar sites require you to be a paid member. If you cannot find too many good articles, check out the articles from Finviz.com.

    Recently, I read an article on AMD and it said it may have good profits in the next two years with the game consoles. The outlook of a company is not shown by any fundamental metric which are far from favorable.

    Following a well-known writer, I bought IBM without doing my due diligence (my fault). It went down more than 15% quickly. You can learn from my mistakes.

2. Research reports from your broker. If you do not find many, open an account with one that provides such reports. Some subscription services such as Value Line provide such reports.

3. Yahoo!Finance board. Most comments are garbage. However, once in a while you find some great insights. Usually you cannot find any info from other sources on tiny companies.

4. The most recent company's financial statements. They are usually available in the company's web site.

5. 10-Ks from Edgar database (www.sec.gov/edgar). Check out new products and its potential competition, key customers, order backlog, research and development and pending lawsuits.

6. Check out the outlook of the sector the company is in and the company itself.

7. Check out its competitors.

8. Some companies are run by stupid people. I received information via my email saying that my mutual fund account could be treated as an abandoned property. I have been cashing dividend checks every year and why it would be considered as an abandoned property. I called them right away to close my account.

    The tall and handsome guy presented articulately how he would turn around JC Penny on TV. I could tell you right away that all his tricks had been tried by other companies such as Sears, and most did not work. The intelligent investor does not care about how handsome, how articulated, how rich his family is and how many advanced degrees from prestigious colleges he possesses. If he does not make sense, do not buy his preaching and his company's stock. [Update. As of 5/2020, J.C. Penny filed for bankruptcy protection. If you had this stock and my book, you would have saved a lot of money minus $10 for my book!]

9. Check out its business model. Some business models do not make business sense and some do. Here are some samples.

- Giving razors makes sense, as the customers have to buy the blades eventually and keep on buying blades for life.

- Supermarket M lowers prices on common merchandises such as Coke and it works. They make money by providing inferior (but profitable to them) products that you cannot compare prices easily such as meat and seafood.

    Eventually there will be a supermarket in my area to satisfy me both in price and quality or at least make a good tradeoff.

12   Sectors to be cautious with

There are many reasons to be very cautious when investing in the following sectors. However, Technical Analysis (a.k.a. charting) would give you more hints than the fundamentals for stocks for these sectors. If the big guys are dumping, most likely Technical Analysis (or the simplest SMA-20) would tell you that.

Loan companies/banks

The financial statements do not show the quality of their loan portfolios. Following this advice, you may be able to skip the banks that melted down in 2007. The peak of Citigroup is $550 and several banks went bankrupt.

Drug (generic is ok)

Understanding the complexities of the drug pipelines, its potential profits for new drugs and the expiration of the current drugs may not worth the effort for most retail investors. In addition, a serious lawsuit and / or a serious problem with a drug could wipe out a good percentage of the stock price. When a drug shows unpromising sign(s) in any trial phase, the stock could plunge and vice versa.

Miners

It is extremely difficult to estimate how much ore (sometimes a miner owns several different types of ores and/or of different grades in the same or different mines) that a company has. It is further complicated by the complexities to extract and transport them. When the total of these costs is greater than its production price, the company will not be profitable. Understanding the market for ore futures is another discipline.

Many mining companies are in foreign countries such as Canada, Australia and countries in South America. Their financial statements of Canada and Australia are more trustworthy than most other emerging countries.

One potential problem of mining companies from many emerging countries is nationalization.

Mining rare earth ore is extremely risky when the profit depends on how China, a major producer of these ores, will price these ores. After China announced the export restrictions on rare earth elements, several non-Chinese companies announced to reopen their mines for rare earths, but few have made any profits as of 2013. Developed countries have stricter environmental regulations.

Coal and eventually oil suffer from the rising use of cleaner energy such as solar and wind.

Insurance companies

Insurance companies profit by:

1. The difference between the total premiums received and the total claims minus expenses in running the company.

2. How well they invest the premiums; you pay your premiums earlier than you may collect from any claims.

They can protect the profits in #1 by restricting claims by natural disasters such as earthquakes and by re-insuring. However, a bad disaster could wipe out a lot of their profits.

Even if the insurance company shows you its investment portfolio, most of us, the retail investors, do not have the time and expertise to analyze it.

Emerging countries (not a sector)

Their financial statements especially from small companies cannot be trusted, and many countries use different accounting standards. Emerging countries are where the economic growth is. I trade FXI, an ETF, rather than individual Chinese companies. I have lost a lot in small Chinese companies due to frauds and politics. To check out whether the stock is an ADR, try ADR.COM (https://www.adr.com/).

Stocks with low volumes (not a sector)

Most likely you pay a high spread to trade these stocks. They can be manipulated easier. I had a hard time trying to sell a stock owned by a few owners.

For simplicity, I trade stocks with the average daily trade volume over 6,000 shares (double it if the price is $2 or less). A better way could be by calculating the percent of your trade quantity / average daily trade volume; it would reduce the effect of penny stocks that have larger volumes due to the low prices.

Good business and bad business

Banking is a good business in a growing economy. My deposit in them makes virtually zero interest, and they loan the same money making 3%. If they are more cautious in loaning, they should make good profits.

Restaurant is an easy business to run, but it is very hard to make good money. With the rising of minimal wages, it will get even tougher. That could be the reason for so many coupons today. The high-end restaurants are doing better due to the rising stock market. The pandemic of 2020 would wipe out a lot of small restaurants.

Retailing is a tough business. Look at the top 10 retailers 15 years ago, I can only find two including Macy's that are still surviving. Most are either went bankrupt or being acquired. Even Macy's was not in good financial shape. Amazon is the killer.

Airlines are a tough business. You can tell by the average increase in fares in the last 10 years. It cannot even beat inflation. They have to charge you for everything. The next frontier charge is the rest room (especially for long-distance flights). Now I understand why they call themselves "Frontier Air". As of 2014, it is quite profitable due to mergers and lower fuel cost. The pandemic of 2020 may be the toughest time for airlines. As of 5/2020, Boeing has many serious troubles and they can only survive with a bailout from the government.

There are several software companies that produce software such as the virus detecting programs and tax preparation software. The customers faithfully buy new versions every year. That's great business.

Afterthoughts

As of 8/2013, is the emerging market oversold?
http://seekingalpha.com/article/1658252-have-emerging-markets-gotten-oversold

When an index of an emerging market is up by 10% and the currency exchange rate to USD is down by 20%, then it is not profitable for us.

13   Mysteries of P/E

If you believe you can make good money by selecting stocks with low P/Es solely, dream on. If it were that easy, there would be no poor folks. However, buying fundamentally sound companies would reduce the risk and improve the chance of its appreciation.

P/E is the most misunderstood indicator. To me, it is the most useful one among all metrics if it is properly used. Earnings are the key to stock appreciation and P/E measures its value. To illustrate on P/E, you pay a million for a hot-dog cart in NYC. Even if its earnings increase year after year, you will never recoup your investment as you have paid too much even for a good business.

"Buy stocks with P/E below 15 and earnings positive" is not true in many cases. P/E growth (PEG) should be considered at least as a prospect of the company. Many retailers were destroyed by Amazon and many newspapers were destroyed by Facebook and Google. Which sector do you want to buy: the sector in up trending or the dying sector even with a better P/E?

Most old books on value are based on old industries that are no longer applicable in today's market. Read these books but ask the above question.

Better definition

P/E should be inverted as E/P, which is termed as Earnings Yield. Earnings Yield is easy to be compared and understood. It takes care of negative earnings for screening stocks and ranking (comparing stocks with the better P/E first). If you sort P/E in ascending order, your order will be wrong with the negative earnings but right with E/P.

It is usually compared to a 10-year Treasury bill yield (or 30 years) or a CD rate. If the stock has 5% earnings yield and your one-year CD is 1%, then it beats the CD by 4% in absolute numbers and four times better. However, the CD is virtually risk free (with deposit amount limits in most banks). Earning yield is an estimated guess and it may not materialize.

Many ways to predict E/P
- Based on the last 12 months. Project it to the Forward E/P. It is also called the last twelve month E/P.

- Based on analysts' educated guesses. Guesses may not materialize. Based on my experience, the expected usually predicts better than the one based on the last 12 months. This is the one I use most and many investing subscriptions provide this Forward P/E (same as the Expected P/E) or expected E/P.

Usually I do not trust the analyst's opinions due to their conflict of interest. However, the earnings estimate is my exception.

- Based on the last month or the last quarter. Latest information could be better for predictions. However, they are not good for seasonal businesses such as the retail where most sales are done during the Christmas season.
- Besides the Pow PE described later, I take the average of the earnings yield EY as:

The Avg. EY = (EY from the last twelve month + Expected EY + EY from the current month of prior year) / 3

It averages out using figures from the past, the present and the future. If no one has used it, I claim shamelessly it is my original idea.

Best E/P could not be the best

Very high E/P could be signs of troubles ahead such as a lawsuit pending, fraud, etc. If you find companies E/P over 50%, it means two years' profits could be equal to the entire cost of the company! I can tell you right away that they probably smell fishy unless you believe that there is a free lunch in life.

However, from time to time, some bargains do exist due to certain conditions, or the Wall Street is just wrong about the company. I found one in my year-end screen and that gave me huge return. You need to find out whether they are bargains or traps. When the E/P is low (sometimes even negative) but is improving fast, it could mean big profits for you. Fundamentalists may miss this opportunity in the early stages due to the unfavorable E/P, but it could be the most profitable time to buy. Sometimes, it could be a turnaround.

During a recession, most good companies have a hard time in promoting new products as the consumers are thrifty. At the same time, it usually is the best time to develop products if they have enough cash to finance them. In this case, there will be no alarm even with negative earnings. The only alarm is when a company cannot meet the debt obligations.

Some companies can manipulate earnings via dirty tricks in accounting. It could make this year look really good, but it is harder or even impossible to continue the same trick for many years. Check out the footnotes in the financial statement.

E/P and PEG

For value investing, E/P is usually used and the higher the better. Watch out when it is extraordinarily high.

PEG (P/E growth) measures the rate of improving P/E. '1' is supposed to be neutral to most investors. When it is below 1, it is undervalued, and vice versa.

PEG = (P/E) / Earnings Growth Rate

They have a similar problem with P/E with negative earnings.

Which of the following two stocks do you want to buy based on their historical earning yields and earnings growth?

1. A stock that has a 10% earnings yield with no earnings growth.
2. A stock that has an 8% earnings yield with 50% earnings growth.

If the earnings growth continues, in next year the second stock should pay 12%, substantially better than the first stock. This is another reason we should use forward earnings rather than historical earnings.

PEG may give a low value for companies that pay high dividends. To correct it,

PEG = (P/E)/ (Earning Growth Rate + Dividend Yield)

When the general market favors growth stocks, weigh more on growth metrics including PEG. I claim no credit on the adjusted PEG.

Fundamental metrics

E/P is one of the metrics you should use but not exclusively. If the earning yield is high but the % of debt is high too, then a good bargain may not be as good as it appears to be.

Some other metrics may not be easily found in the financial statements such as the intangibles, insider buying, pension obligations, trade secrets, losing market share, brand name, customers' loyalty, etc. It is interesting that most metrics change its ability to predict from time to time.

P/E variations

There are other P/E variations like Shiller P/E (same as CAPE and PE10). Shiller P/E can also be used to track the current market valuation. It is controversial and its value is easily misinterpreted. Hence, use it as a reference only unless you understand all its issues. I prefer to use two year average of the P/E instead of 10 as I believe the market changes too much over a ten year span. Currently Shill P/E does not work that well as before. It is due to the excessive printing of money.

Compare a company's current P/E to its average P/E in the last 5 years. Also compare it to the average value of the companies in the same industry. The average P/E for high-tech companies is different from supermarkets for example. They are available from Fidelity.

P/E is more reliable for a group of stocks (SPY for example) instead of individual stocks which have too many other metrics and intangibles to deal with. When you compare the total return of an ETF to a corresponding index, you need to add the respective dividends to the index to ensure a fair comparison of total returns. As of this writing, the S&P 500 is paying about a 2% dividend.

EV/EBITDA is another way to measure the value of a company. This metric has its advantages and disadvantages over P/E. It includes other important data such as cash and debt. EBITDA/EV is equivalent to E/P including other mentioned metrics. I prefer to use it over E/P. Some sites do not provide it if the earnings is negative. The disadvantage to me is it does not use expected earnings. This ratio can be found under Yahoo!Finance.

Garbage in, garbage out
I do not trust most financial statements from emerging countries, especially the smaller companies. Watch out for fraudulent data. Most metrics can be manipulated. Recently I have a US stock that lost 18% in one day due to the SEC's investigation of its financial data.

The announced earnings may not be reflected in the financial statements that you use from the web. Ensure your data is up-to-date by checking the date of the financial statements. Seeking Alpha has transcripts for the earnings announcements that would save you a trip to attend the companies' quarterly meetings.

Sector and entire market
You can find the value of a sector using the P/E of an ETF for that sector. It is similar for the market. For example, use SPY (an ETF simulating the S&P 500 index). If it is lower than the average (15 to me), then most likely the market is good value and a buy signal. It is one of the many hints for market timing.

Where to use P/E

Each highlight of the following corresponds to one of my books. Click it for the description of the strategy.

My book on top-down approach starts with a safe market, then sector analysis, fundamental analysis, intangible analysis and optionally technical analysis. P/E is one of the many metrics in fundamental analysis.

There are many styles of investing. In general, fundamental analysis is important when you hold the stock longer.

- P/E is important in Long-Term Swing, Dividend Investing, Retirees and Conservative Strategies.
- My max value is 20 and 25 for tech companies. I ignore it if they have high potential for appreciation that could be indicated by insider purchases. However, many unknown companies then had a P/E over 50. Tesla had a P/E over 1,000 at one time.
- P/E is moderately important in Short-Term Swing and Sector Rotation.
- P/E is the least important in Momentum Strategy and Day Trading.

Summary
Again, one metric should not dictate the reason to trade a stock. Compare the company P/E to its industry average and its own five-year average. In addition, many industries have cycles. If you buy it at the peak of the industry, the P/E may mislead you. Besides fundamental analysis, you need to consider intangible analysis and time the entry / exit point by using technical analysis. Intangible analysis evaluates information that cannot be summarized into numeric metrics such as a lawsuit pending.

True P/E
"EV/EBITDA" is available from Yahoo!Finance and other sources. The true EY is "1/Ture PE". I call it "True" for the lack of a better term as it represents the financial situation of the company better. This could be the most important metric for many.

Earnings can be manipulated. For example, the company management can lower the P/E ratio by buying back its stocks. In this case the earnings per share is boosted but in reality there is no change in the company's financial fundamentals. The true P/E takes into consideration the reduced cash. EBITBA stands for "Earnings Before Interest, Taxes, Depreciation, and Amortization".

Be careful when EV or "EBITDA" is negative. Most likely you should avoid the stocks with a negative EV.

Yahoo!Finance usually leaves EV/EVITDA blank for financial institutions such banks, loan companies and REITS. In this case, use forward earnings yield (= 1 / Forward P/E or Pow Earnings Yield described next.

Pow P/E

You should use the described "EV/EBITDA" and hence "Pow P/E" can be ignored. There are some cases that Pow P/E is better: 1. "EV/EBITDA" may not be available for reasons such as negative asset and 2. Use of Forward Earnings instead of Earnings based on the last twelve months. The following is an exercise on how I simulate it from Finviz.com with metrics that are readily available.

I modified P/E to take care of cash and debts. I use my last name due to being easier to distinguish from P/E and it has nothing to do with my ego.

Pow P/E = (P - Cash per Share + Debt per Share) / (Earning - Interest gained per share - Interest paid per share)

Pow Earnings Yield = 1 / Pow P/E

Here is a comparison of E/P (Earnings Yield), Expected Earnings Yield (Forward E /P), True Yield (EBITD/EV) and Pow Earning Yields, which is based one Forward (Expected) Earnings as of 10/14/2021.

	CARS	MPAA
Earnings Yield	1%	7%
Expected Earnings Yield	12%	12%
True Yield	13%	11%
Pow Earnings Yield	5%	9%

P/E is not always important

The following is my test from 1/2/2020 to 10/14/2020. RSP is similar to SPY except that the stocks in the S&P 500 index are equally weighed. EY (= E/P) is Expected Earnings Yield and there is no stocks with EY less than 0. DY is Dividend Yield. GPE is the growth of P/E. As in my book, I use annualized returns and dividends are not included. This test does not mean a lot, but it tells us what these metrics behave during this period, or it indicates **Value is not a good metric in this period**, and it may indicate momentum is better in this period. Most big winners start as small companies with **high P/E** (from 30 to 100). Many of them have important technologies or special systems that would change the world such as Microsoft, Facebook, Amazon and Walmart to name a few. Their sales have increased substantially year after year.

Examples of not depending on low P/Es. Before the financial crisis in 2008, P/Es of most bank stocks had 10-year low. After they announced the earnings, P/Es of many of them surged to over 100 and the stock prices suffered losses of more than 80% within 12 months. The stock price of Bethlehem Steel with P/E of 2 at one time went to zero. Need to find out why the stock is so cheap via intangible analysis and qualitative analysis.

The following is very rough testing and there are many limitations in the database. However, the conclusion is quite convincing to me and some are opposite to the contrary beliefs. For example, I expected the higher EY the better, but not in this test.

	Ann. Return	Indicator	Comment
RSP 500 All	-2%		
EY (top 10)	-54%	Bad	Contrary
GPE (top 10)	-20%	Bad	Contrary
Select All or top 100.			
DY = 0	16%	Good	
DY (top 100)	-19%	Bad	
DY / 1 and 2	2%		
EY 3 to 4	15%	Good	Second best

EY 2 to 3	6%	Good	Third best
EY 1 to 2	31%	Good	Best
EY 0 to 1	-39%	Bad`	

I use some metrics from a service I subscribe to that are not included here. Two major metrics of this subscription have a return of around 20%. Most subscriptions including the free Fidelity (to some extent) give you three composite scores: Total, Fundamental and Timing. I wish to check out the recent predictability of Fidelity's Equity Summary Score if they have a historical database. Most of them take out the delisted and /or bankrupt companies in their databases.
Link: P/E: https://www.youtube.com/watch?v=4KkTGx2bK_4

Section III: Trading stocks

Introduction

The simple formula to make money is to find value stocks and wait for the market to realize their values. Only buy the market is not risky. Most successful investors are doing this.

The book value of a stock is simply the net worth of a company (= Assets − Liabilities). When the stock price is higher than the book value per share (i.e. 'Stock Price / Book Price' > 1), it is over-valued. When this ratio is more than 2 or less than 0.5, you have to be cautious. When it is way underpriced, there may be a critical reason.

Intrinsic Value includes the intangibles such as patents. However, both the Book Value and Intrinsic Value have not been convincing as predictors to me from my tests. Briefly, describe some basic but important metrics here.

- Expected Earning Yield (E/P). The future appreciation depends on future earnings and the current price of the stock (you do not want to overpay). I prefer a range from 5% to 30%.
- Growth of Earnings and growth of sales. Compare them to their numbers in the same quarter last year. I prefer 10% or higher.
- How good is the management? Measured by ROE. I prefer 10% or higher.

- How safe it the company? Measured by 'Debt/Equity'. I prefer less than .5 (same as 50%). However, some industries are debt intensive.

These are the ratios readily available from many sites including Finviz.com except reversing P/E for earning yield. There is no need to dig into the complicated financial statements to start.

The predictability of most metrics changes according to the current market conditions. Monitor their performance and act accordingly. I prefer E/P but Earnings/Sales had better predictability in my last test.

Filler: A nightmare?

I got a call from Buffett asking me to lead their stock research.
I asked him why for a nobody; you may be asking the same question. No kidding.

He told me that he should have read my book Scoring Stocks to buy Apple instead of IBM in May, 2013. It would save his company millions of dollars minus $10 for my book. Not to mention the market timing technique that had worked in the last two major market plunges.

I told him, "OK, I'll beat your mediocre returns of the last 5 years."
He said, "You can do better than that and at least beat SPY. If you do so, no one will be that stupid to leave my fund and pay the hefty capital gain taxes."

I told him, "I cannot beat the market as you are the market especially after your expensive fees. In addition, I do not know how to avoid day traders from riding my wagon in trading. Also most of my big profits were made in small stocks that your fund cannot trade besides owning the company."

I woke up trembling. I'm glad it is only a nightmare.

1   Order prices

Market orders

It is simply trading the stock at the prevailing market price. Place market orders only when it is necessary as stocks price can easily be manipulated especially on stocks with low trading volumes. To avoid manipulations, do not place market orders after hours.

However, in a rising market, many fast rising stocks can only be bought via market orders. Many winners never take a breather on their way up. In this case, you can only buy the stock via market orders.

Consider bid and ask. A 'bid' is the price a potential buyer would like to buy while the 'ask' is a potential seller would like to sell. Your market price is usually the worst price in either case, but it is a guarantee that you would trade the stock. A large spread would mean that it would take a longer time to use a limit order and/or the trade volume of the stock is small.

In my momentum portfolio on 11/2013, I placed a sell price for GERN far higher than the market price. Surprisingly I sold it for this price making an annualized return of 1,176% for holding it for 21 days. When there are few or no other sellers for the stock, the market price would be the price you set. If I cannot sell it in the next 9 days (30 days is my holding period for momentum stocks), I would set it lower. Update: One year later, GERN lost 29%.

Sensible discounts

I prefer to buy the stock at the price closest to the last trade price (to most it is the market price) via a limit order. I seldom lose buying these orders. Sometimes I use the day's lowest price to buy (or the highest to sell) plus a penny (or minus a penny for sell prices to sell).

My other purchase strategy is using 0.15% or 0.25% less than the current prices for stocks I really want. For some promising stocks, I buy them at almost the market price and then place another order on the same stock at 0.5% less than the last traded price (and sometimes 2% depending on the current market trend).

We all want to buy less and sell at higher prices. However, if the trade price is too far away from the current market price (such as 5% from the market price), these trades may never be executed. I have had a long list of buy orders that were not executed and turned out to be big gainers. Learn from my bad experiences.

Use a good discount (such as 10% from the market price) if you believe the market, the sector or the stock will dip by 10%. After you bought the stock, you place a sell order 10% more than the price you paid for it hoping the stock will return to the original price and you pocket 10%. Wishful thinking! However, it has happened to me several times primarily due to temporary market dips.

It works when there is a correction and/or the stock is very volatile. It is usually within the 5% range to take advantage of these situations, not the 10% as described. For a 10% plunge, it usually is due to some serious problem of the company surfacing. One common reason is not meeting its earnings expectation and in this case it usually continues its downward trend.

Larger discounts on a falling market
During a falling market (or a mild correction), 3% less than the current prices for buy orders may be fine for some stocks (use 5% for volatile stocks). To illustrate, I placed about 10 of these orders over the last two months during a market dip. Most of the orders were filled. When the market is plunging, do not buy any stock.

Caterpillar and Cisco were some of my buys at these discounts. They were in my watch list to buy. Initially these shares often fall even lower as the trend was downward. As of 12/18/12, CAT earned me from 3% and 14% (bought in 6/12 and 7/12) and CSCO bought in 7/14/12 returned about 34%. My original objective: Buy deeply-valued stocks, wait and sell them when the economy returns.

When you predict the market will dip by 5%, set your buy orders accordingly. Again, predictions are just educated guesses. From my experience, they work most of the time but not all of the time.

On the day of the earnings announcement, the fluctuation of the stock is usually high. Check any change in the earnings estimate before the announcement and act accordingly. Zacks is supposed to be a useful tool to predict earnings estimates. Do not leave orders during the earnings announcement dates, which can be found in Finviz. When the earning turns out to be good, the stock price surges and your order will not be executed. When the earnings are bad, the stock price will plunge usually and you most likely over-payed.

Option expiration dates usually cause more volatility. Retail investors do not have to be concerned except you may use wider stops. In theory, dividend days have little effect on the stock price as it will be lowered by the dividend amount.

High volume of a stock could mean opportunity

High volume usually increases the stock price volatility. If the volatility of a stock increases substantially (such as doubling its average daily volume), there could be important news on the company, recommendation changes from a major analyst or trading by the institutional investors. It usually takes the institutional investors a week to trade a stock with their sizable positions.

Many times it is started by the insiders who know about the breaking news of a stock before it is publicized. Some investment services / sites specialize in identifying the increasing volumes on these stocks.

Because day traders do not want to leave any open positions overnight, higher volatility occurs at the end of the day. It is the same on the day (usually on Friday) when the options are expiring.

Monitor your trade prices

You cannot tell whether you are paying a fair price without keeping a record. To illustrate, you're paying 1% less than the market prices in buying stocks. You may have missed buying some winners. If the 1% you saved is smaller than the appreciation of the stocks you would have bought at market prices, then you should adjust the buy prices to 0.5% less than the market price and monitor again.

Market trend makes a difference too. When the market is trending up, buying any stock would most likely be profitable and usually the purchase orders with higher discounts will not be executed.

Follow the same logic on sell orders. Need to have at least 25 stock purchases (and potential purchases) to make the conclusion meaningful. If you do not trade a lot, you will not have enough data to verify. As described, I prefer not to place an order during the earnings announcement dates which can be found in Finviz.com. If you cannot buy the stock, consider to use market order the next day. With most brokers offer no commission trades, the "All or none" option is not valid.

Good prospects

When you find gems especially those stocks that are followed by analysts, buy them at market prices and consider doubling the bet if you are really sure you have a winner. From my super stock screens, I spotted NHTC. I placed several bets and one market order. All of them were NOT executed except with the market order. At the end of the day NHTC is up 18% and my executed order is up 14%. I did not have the best buy but made a good profit. NHTC was on its way to a huge appreciation and I sold it too early. I have earned not to sell a winner and protect the profit with a stop.

Lower the buy for risky stocks (if the beta from Finviz is greater than 1 for example) even if they have good fundamentals.

Quality over quantity

If your time is limited, spend all the time on researching one stock one at a time. However, you need to own at least 3 stocks (more stocks for a large portfolio) for your diversification purposes.

Double your normal purchase position on stocks that look great after the research. For risky stocks that look good, you may want to halve your normal purchase position to cut down on the risk. If you are less risk tolerant, do not buy risky stocks at all. My results are not conclusive on risky stocks but I do get a good sleep.

A recent example

Recently I sold EA with $1 more than my order price but $2 less than the current price of the day, which was the earnings announcement day. I do recommend not placing orders right before the earnings announcement day for the stock. If the earnings are good, you do not get all the profit as in this real example; my broker did get me $1 more. If the earnings are bad, you will not sell it any way. It is the same for buying stocks.

Afterthoughts

- Besides luck, the smart investor never sells at the peak but usually within 10% of the peak. No one can predict the peaks consistently.

- I made mistakes like most of you. One time my buy price was higher than the last price executed. Luckily my broker adjusted it to the right price but I may not be that lucky next time. Several times I switched the buy price and sell price by mistake. One time it was due to my boss coming by that forced me to enter my order hastily. Try to avoid the first hour of a trade session.
- Some experts do not suggest their clients to buy stocks on the way down. With respect, I offer opposing arguments.

  - It is fine to buy them on the way down, if you have the conviction that the company or the economy will recover.
  - No one knows where the bottom is, but averaging down could be beneficial if the company or the economy can recover. Check why its stock price is falling and whether the company can fix its problems. Some major problems are only temporary or easy to fix.
  - Most of my big profits are made by buying close to the bottom prices on stocks that have a good potential to recover.
  - Many value stocks are on sale when the market dips. The most favorable time is in the Early Recovery, a phase in the market cycle defined by me.

Links
Selling short:
http://en.wikipedia.org/wiki/Short_%28finance%29
Short squeeze:
http://en.wikipedia.org/wiki/Short_squeeze
Fidelity Video: Stop Loss.
https://www.fidelity.com/learning-center/trading/trailing-stops-video

2   Stop loss & flash crash

You can limit your stock loss with stops. There are some incidents where you do not always want to use a stop loss.

- Flash crash (May 6, 2010 also August 2015).
  It would turn your stops into market orders that could be substantially lower than your stop prices. Some brokers offer stop limits, but they do not guarantee the orders will be executed.

  The better way is a "mental stop" (my term). You do not place a stop order but place a market order to sell when your stock falls below a pre-defined price. During flash crashes, you do not want to place the market orders to sell but place orders to buy from your watch list.

  I bought some stocks at more than 10% discount during the flash crash (actually I could buy them even at better discounts) and within a week most had returned to the prices as before the flash crash.

  Placing buy orders with huge discounts to the market prices works better for volatile stocks. You should cancel the unexecuted trades before the weekends / holidays and reenter them afterwards to avoid unexpected events that may affect the stock prices.

  Avoid trading drug and bio tech companies with huge differences to the market prices. High tech is a good sector for this purpose and fluctuating 10% in this sector is more of a norm than an exception. Buying an ETF at 5% discount is a better bet than buying specific stocks from my experience.

- My experience with 911.
  I sold many stocks due to stop orders during 911. The market came back in the next three days and I missed the recovery from the stocks that were sold and did not buy back them in time.

- If your stocks are rising, you need to adjust the stop loss prices accordingly. To illustrate- in maintaining a 10% stop loss, your stop is at 90 when the current price is 100. When the stock price rises to 200, it should be adjusted to $180 (10% less than the current price). It is also called a trailing stop. Need to review these rising stocks, and change the stop price periodically (one week to one month depending on how volatile is the stock)).

Most brokers allow you to enter most trades "Good till Cancelled". Even for that there is an expiration date such as 6 months for Fidelity. Fidelity's trades for Short Sell expire by the end of the trade session. Check your broker's current policy.

- Risky markets.
  When the market is risky, you may want to use a stop loss. To prevent another flash crash, you may want to use a 'mental' market order. It is not perfect, as it requires constant watching of the market.

  There are many investing services and sites that give you the 'right' prices for a stop loss. Basically it depends on how volatile are the specific stocks. The chartists will tell you under normal conditions stocks are trading between the resistance line and the support line. Use the stop loss just below the resistance line to avoid the stop order from being executed due to the volatility of the stock.

  For simplicity as I have too many stocks in my portfolio, I use a percent. In the old days, it was recommended 8% or so below the prices you paid. In today's volatile market, I recommend 12%.

- Risky stocks.
  A stop loss is the only way that you can limit your loss for big drop (such as 25%). Affimax lost 85% of its stock value in one day with the news that three of its patients died.

- Low-volume stocks.
  The market order could drive the prices right down as there are few buyers in low-volume stocks. If there is only one buyer, he will buy with the best price for him (or the worst price to the seller).

Unless I have good reasons, I would skip the low-volume stocks. I define low-volume: If my buy amount is higher than 1% of the average daily amount (= average daily volume * stock price).

- Beta.
  Stocks may be more volatile than the market. Beta is used to measure its volatility. The market can be measured by the S&P500 index. If the beta of a stock is 1, its volatility is the same as the market. If it is 1.2, it is 20% more volatile.

  Set a lower stop loss for volatile stocks to prevent stocks from selling due to regular fluctuations.

Afterthoughts

Let me show you my bitter experience. The following are 5 stocks I wanted to buy and the average return was quite good.

Stocks	Return
URI	63%
GMCR	572%
MTW	186%
PII	-74%
TSCO	-127%
Avg.	124%

I placed buy orders at 5% less than the market prices as most 'bargain' investors do. I bought both of the two losers but no winners. The winners never took a breather on its way up, but the losers went down. I did buy GMCR via a market order in my momentum strategy in a separate account.

3 Covered calls

For basic descriptions on a covered call from Wikipedia, click here or enter (http://en.wikipedia.org/wiki/Covered_call) in your browser.

It is like collecting rent from the apartment you bought. The difference is that the renter has an option to buy the apartment at a preset time and price.

The rent is quite substantial if you do good planning. To start with, you want to buy stocks that have a market to sell. Usually they are large companies with high trading volumes.

Since one contract is for 100 shares of a stock, you cannot sell a covered call on 50 shares of a stock. On the other hand, when you have 1,000 stocks, the commission of 10 contracts would be more than the cost of 1 contract depending on your broker's schedule.

It is time consuming to keep track of the covered calls but it is well worth your time and effort. If the stock price exceeds the strike price of your covered call, you may want to buy the same shares back, so you would not miss any further appreciation of this stock.

However, if it is in a taxable account and you have a loss in a forced sell, do not buy it back otherwise the tax loss is not allowed (i.e. a wash sale) for the year as of 2016. When the contract expires, you may want to start another contract on the same stock if the stock has not been sold.

Covered calls do have their disadvantages such as higher commission rates and sometimes forcing you to sell at a higher tax rate for short-term capital gains in taxable accounts. It is avoidable by using covered calls on stocks that are qualified for long-term capital gains. In addition, you need to buy them back when they increase in price beyond your strike price or lose its potential to appreciate further. Using another put could keep you from not losing any gains beyond the strike price. However, I prefer to use my time in more productive ways and this insurance is not cheap. One's opinion.

One company advertises their techniques using covered calls which could give their users 3 to 6% monthly returns. If you believe in this fantasy, you do not need this book. There is no free lunch.

My recent experience

I sold Netflix covered calls with the strike price about 2% higher and a 3% premium (from my memory) but the price shot up 12% higher in one day, so I was potentially losing 7% profit. However, it turned out to be a good experience as Netflix went downhill later (8/2012).

Normally I prefer to sell covered options for stocks with a quantity from 100 to 600 shares (i.e. 1 to 6 contracts) for the longest time (about 2-3 months). Some non-volatile and small stocks are not candidates to write covered calls on. Some stocks are not optionable. Typically high-tech stocks have a higher premium to be collected as their stock prices fluctuate more. The right stocks can generate 10% or even more a year in addition to the fluctuations of the stock prices.

In general, if I feel the market will be down for the period, I use covered calls especially for stocks holding over one year (unless I have short-term loss to offset any short-term gains) in taxable accounts. Watch out for any tax change that may affect your total return.

Recently I attended a sales pitch on a 3-day training course on a strategy for making 24% per year and it is quite possible especially with the S&P 500 returns about the same. I wish it were available to me 15 years ago. It seems to be too good to be true.

How to sell covered calls

First you need to open an account with your broker and apply to trade options including covered calls.

Check how your broker charges commissions. Ask how much they charge for one contract and 10 contracts of a stock.

The covered call is an agreement to sell the rights to the buyer of the stock at the strike price for a specific date range (a.k.a. expiration date). Typically options expire on Fridays.

You need to write covered calls on the stocks you already own. One contract is 100 shares of stocks. Check out the option chain to select the price, expiration period and the strike price. Normally, the strike price should be higher than the current market price. You may want to have an expiration date 2 weeks or longer. When the contract is expiring in a few days, the contract has little value and most likely the small 'rent' is not worth the risk and the commission.

When the covered call is sold, you receive the 'rent' immediately and any dividend during the 'rental' period.

When the option is 'called' due to a price rise above the strike price, your stock will be sold and you will have to pay the regular commission.

At this point, evaluate the stock to check whether you want to buy it back. If the stock surges, you may have to pay a higher price – thus losing the extra appreciation. In addition, you may have to pay a higher capital gains tax if it is held less than the required period for long-term capital gains in a taxable account.

Note. Notice that some stocks are not optionable and/or not practical to write options on. Most brokers charge a flat rate for the first contract (such as $7) and an incremental fee for each additional contract. Shop around as the fees vary if you write a lot of covered calls.

The best stocks for covered calls are large US companies with a large average volume. The option (a.k.a. the 'rent') pays better for volatile companies such as high-tech companies. From my rough estimates for illustration purposes, the annualized return on covered calls for AAPL is 25% and C is 12% after commission.

4   *When to sell a stock*

There are many reasons to sell a stock as follows.

Personal

1. Has met my targets/objectives.
    It could be a 10% gain in a very short-term swing, x% return in
    4 months for a short-term swing or y% gain after a year for
    long-term trades. Define x and y depending on your risk
    tolerance and how often you trade.

    I bought 4 stocks in one day during the August, 2015 correction
    and placed sell orders with 10% more than my purchase prices.
    I sold one in a day and another one within a month. This is my
    strategy for correction – sometimes it works and sometimes it
    does not.

    Never look back. Do not blame yourself when the prices are
    better than your trade prices. When the market is volatile, use a
    higher percent of the current prices. Be disciplined. Stay on the
    same strategy and detach yourself from emotions.

2. Realize that we have made a mistake. Do not let your ego block
    your eyes. It could be due to bad analysis, bad, data, unexpected
    fraud, lawsuits, and/or unforeseeable events that you have no
    control of. It is better to get out with a small loss. I prefer a 25%
    loss as a threshold for long-term strategies and a 10% (or less for
    some strategies) loss for short-term strategies.

    We have to ensure whether it is a mistake or not. If the 'mistake'
    is just bad luck or due to conditions we cannot possibly predict
    or control, then it is not a mistake. If it is a mistake, learn from
    it. When we diversify, one bad loss should not cause a big dent
    in our portfolios. The stop loss is a good tool most of the time
    except when there is a flash crash.

    If the criteria have been faithfully followed and it does not work
    well, check out whether your criteria are wrong, or it does not
    work on the current market conditions.

3. When we have too many stocks in the same sector, we will want to replace some stocks to better diversify our portfolios.

    When the sector is rising, we want to weigh more on that sector at the expense of diversification, and vice versa. Set a limit of how many sectors you should hold.

4. Need cash for living expenses.

5. To reduce a tax burden by selling some losers. Tax consideration should not be the primary reason for selling. Take advantage of the favorable tax treatment for long-term capital gains. In short, sell losers within the short term limit (currently a year), and sell winners after 365 days; check the current tax laws.

    Harvest tax losses. Sell losers and buy back similar stocks (or same stock after 31 days to avoid wash sale). It is not too clear in which you can buy back the same loser in your children's account under the current tax law.

6. To take advantage of a lower tax. In 2013, we can pay virtually zero (except the increase of tax on social security payment) Federal income taxes on long-term capital gains when our income is below a specific tax bracket (15% as of 2015). Check out the current tax laws. Evaluate the sold winners for a possible buy back.

Market Timing

7. When the market or the sector plunges, sell stocks or stocks within the sector.

    For temporary peaks, evaluate which stocks in your portfolio to sell based on fundamentals. The objective is to raise cash for buying opportunities.

Deteriorating appreciation potential

8. There may be some stocks that have a better appreciation potential than the ones you currently own. Churning the portfolio by replacing better stocks may cost some brokerage

commissions (some are free today) and taxes for taxable accounts, but it improves the quality and the appreciation potential for the entire portfolio.

9. The company's fundamentals have changed for the worse. If you use a scoring system, compare the current score with the score you actually bought the stock for. Apple is a good example from 2013 to 2015. Buy when the fundamentals are good and sell when they are not.

   The basic fundamentals are expected P/E, the quarter-to-quarter earnings growth rate / the sales growth rate, and Debt /Equity.

   When your stocks have passed the peak and started to decline, sell them. When they are heading to bankruptcy, sell them fast.

Hints that the fundamentals are degrading

Evaluate the stocks you own at least every 6 months and check their daily news at least once a week that can be easily done using Seeking Alpha's portfolio function.

- The cash flow is decreasing fast. Cash flow is not a particularly good predicative indicator for appreciation, but a good indicator on whether the company will survive. This metric is very hard to manipulate.

- A new or pending lawsuit. Check out how serious the lawsuit is and be aware that a minor lawsuit can be ignored. Companies always sue against each other.

- A big drop in sales. Do not be alarmed when a new product, or a new drug is going to replace a major product. Compare sales to the same quarter of prior year to avoid seasonal fluctuations (Q-to-Q info I available from Finviz.com).

- Management deteriorates- One hint is the deteriorating ROE from the last quarter.

- The extravagant life style of the CEO and the many easy loans to officers.

- Poor operations. They include recalls of products such as the GM recall on ignition switches, product secrets being stolen and customers' credit card info being stolen. Boeing's 747-Max is a warning call.

- A successful product from the competitor, or the current product is losing its market share, or becoming a low-profit commodity.

- Insiders and/or institutional investors are dumping the companies' stocks far more than the averages (2% for me) especially in heavy volumes and by more than one insider.

  - Have more than one insider dumping a lot of the stock within a month and no insider purchase in that month.

  - Have more than one insider decrease their holdings by more than 10%.

- When the SEC or any government agency pays attention to a company, it usually means bad news.

- Deceptive accounting practices have been discovered.

- Increasing receivable and/or inventory at an alarming rate.

- Earnings have been restated too many times.

- Short percentage is increasing fast – someone found something wrong with the company.

- The invalidity of 'one-time charges'.

- Abnormal return rate of the company's pension fund comparing to the average of the companies in the same sector.

- Too many and too costly reconstructing charges.

- The entire stock market is plunging as indicated by our chart in detecting market crashes.

- The stock price does not move up with good news. It shows the price has peaked.

- The accumulation amount is far less than the sold amount. When the stock price is up, the accumulation is less than the sold stocks when the stock price was down the last time. It indicates that no more accumulation is ahead and hence the stock will be down most likely.

Afterthoughts
- Another article on this topic.
  http://buzz.money.cnn.com/2013/04/05/stocks-sell/
  An article from Investopedia. Nothing new but it is worth having the same second opinion.
  http://www.investopedia.com/financial-edge/0412/5-tips-on-when-to-sell-your-stock.aspx
- It also depends on your strategies. I sell most of my stocks in my momentum portfolio within a month. At least one strategy I know of does not keep any stock during the peak stage of the market cycle – the easiest time to make money but also the riskiest time.

  If you use charts for trading, sell the stocks that are below your moving averages or other technical analysis indicators. Personally I do not use charts for making sell decisions due to my limited time.

- Sell when the company is heading into bankruptcy as described before. The red flags are: 1. Negative cash flow. 2. Heavy insiders dumping the stocks. 3. Pending major lawsuit. 4. Fraud from the management.
- Risky periods for a stock.
  Earnings announcement (4 times a year), settling a major lawsuit and/or during a FDA event in approving a drug are risky periods for a stock. A fluctuation more than 5% in either direction is normal. Some use options to buy insurance. Most ignore it. For the majority of the time, heavy insider purchase is a good

indicator. There are rumors (or educated guesses) on earnings before their announcements. Zacks is supposed to be a good subscription for earnings estimates.

Selling a winner

Let the profit rise and at the same time protect your profit. Tesla quadrupled its value in 6 months. Examples abound such as Amazon and Yelp.

You do not want to sell these rocket stocks even if their fundamentals do not make sense. Buffett does not touch these stocks and he usually misses these big gains. However, many of these rocket stocks such as BRRY (Blackberry) will eventually fall losing most of their value. I bet the institutional investors move the market in either direction and usually they read the same analysts' reports. You profit as a contrarian if you have a good reason to act against the herd.

The following example uses a 10% trailing stop. Set the stop at 10% of the current price (i.e. 10% less than the current price), not the purchase price. You need to change the stop when the price rises but do not change it when the price falls. Review your stops every month or more frequently if time allows.

To illustrate, when the stock price rises to 100, set the stop at 90. When the stock price falls to 90, sell the stock at the market price. When the stock price rises to 200, change the stop at 180.

The stop should also be set according to how volatile the stock is. Some stocks are more volatile than others. Most charts show the resistance line. This line assumes the stock price should not fall below this line in normal fluctuations. Set the stop at 2% below this line so your stock will not be stopped out in theory.

To avoid flash crashes, do not place stop orders. Instead, do it mentally (mental stop is my term). When you see that the stock falls below your stop with no sign of a flash crash, sell the stock using a market order.

Of course, there is no bullet-proof scheme. This one should work in the long run. This is my suggestion only, so examine whether it works for you. Small cap and/or stocks with small average volumes fluctuate more.

Examples
I have too many bad examples of selling the stocks too early and sometimes holding them too long.

I made over 40% in a few weeks on ALU, but it went up more than 300% in the next two years. It was acquired in early 2016 by Nokia paying a good premium. I was right that ALU had a lot of valuable patents and I was wrong to dump it when I found out Cisco did not have any intention to acquire it – a big mistake by Cisco and the U.S.

FOSL is another example to teach us to use mental stop loss. FOSL was priced at $33.70 on 1/4/2010. Its fundamentals were just fine with an expected E/P (expected earnings yield) at 6% but decreasing earnings. It gained 115% later in 2010 - not expected.

On 1/3/2011, the expected E/P was still at around 6% and improving earnings. It gained 9% for the year – a little disappointing.

On 1/3/2012, the expected E/P was 7% and a huge earnings growth. Now, we expected a better performance for the year and it did by gaining 20%.

On 1/3/2013, the expected E/P was about 6% and the earnings gain was respectable. It gained 28% to $121. So far, so good.

On 1/2/2014, the E/P and the earnings growth were about the same as in 1/3/2013. However, it lost 7% for the year while SPY (an ETF simulating the market) gained 12%. There was no warning. Did the institutional investors lose the interest of this stock? On 1/2/2015, the E/P was 7% and the earnings growth was about the same as the previous year. It lost 69% (vs. SPY's 0% return with dividends)!

From 1/4/2010 to 1/3/2016, the annualized return of FOSL is 0% (vs. SPY's 13%). Actually, after dividends, SPY should have an annualized return of about 15%. The lessons gained here are:

- Fundamentals (using EP and earnings growth in this example) may not always work. Otherwise, 2015 should have the same gain as 2014.
- The rosy outlook of the stock may be priced in already. When the outlook fails to materialize, the stock tanks.

5   Rocket stocks

There are stocks making yearly highs and continue so for a while. They defy fundamental rules. Among many examples, Tesla appreciated about 400% from 4/2013 to 10/2013. However, when they reverse direction, they may lose more than they have gained. BBRY lost 95% of its value in 4 years after gaining about 30 times in 5 years. Some are manipulated by institution investors. Most have new products that could change the world. When they have unfixable problems such as competing products and/or major pending lawsuits, they will plunge. I call them rocket stocks and they may plunge at the speed they surge.

From my tests on these stocks, they share common metrics. Most of these stocks hitting 52-week highs or close to them can be found in your stock section of the newspaper and many investing sites. Usually their SMA-50%s are higher than their SMA-200%s, which are both available from finviz.com.

The other metrics are stock prices greater than $10 and the market cap is between 3 billion and 8 billion. I would also include 100M to 500M stocks for larger appreciation potential although they are more risky. They should be listed in the major 3 exchanges. These are the stocks institution investors would evaluate (greater than 4B); institution investors drive the market. The volume should at least double the average volume; it is a confirmation. Rating on timing from many investing sites (some are free) are high.

You can alter the above criteria especially on many small drug companies and small high-tech companies. Insider purchase is another good criterion to search for rocket stocks. Avoid bankrupting stocks no matter how high they surge. Do not be greedy as some will return to the original prices and even go to zero. When the institution investors switch to the next rocket stock or sector, these rocket stocks will plunge in prices. As recommended on how to sell rising stocks, use mental (a.k.a. trailing) stops such as 10%. When it falls to 10% of the last time you set the stop, sell it and do not look back. If the market (SPY) loses 10%, it may not be the reason to sell if your rocket stock loses the same. The average holding period of 3 months is the best in my limited testing. However, some rocket stocks do not obey the law of gravity. No one can time the peaks and bottoms consistently.

6   Diversification

LTCM, a hedge fund run by smart people, and Isaac Newton both made one serious mistake about investing. They both bet all in one bet and they lost it big. They were the smartest folks on earth but they violated one basic principle about investing: diversification.

Another example is the potato. Irish made good living in their primary crop: potato. When a virus came, they lost all the potatoes and caused the potato famine.

Diversification improves a portfolio's performance in the long run and it reduces risk. Diversification includes other asset class besides stocks such as oil, gold, cash (yes even cash as a safety net to grasp better opportunities ahead), real estate, etc. However, stocks historically produce the best return. In addition, most stocks are quite liquid as it takes a minute to sell them compared to selling a house for example. You can buy other assets such as gold (GLD), money market funds and real estate (via REITs) via the low-cost ETFs.

When an asset is over-valued, it will return to the average historical value with one or two exceptions. Gold is one exception, but it is partly due to the depreciation of USD and the previous prolonged downfall of gold adjusted to inflation.

Simply put, owning 10 to 15 good stocks with less than three stocks in the same sector (which have to be good sectors to start with) achieves diversification goal for most. When one sector crashes, you still have two more good sectors.

Every one's situation is different:

- Depends on your wealth and your age.
  For younger folks with limited wealth (less than $50,000 to invest), a portfolio of 3 stocks (preferably most in ETFs) in different sectors or one diversified ETF could be enough. Your objective about investing is saving money for a down payment for a house, paying your loans including college loans and/or improving your earning power by taking classes.

Retirees may want to maintain a larger percentage of your holdings in cash and/or invested in bonds (long-term bonds could be very risky when the interest rates is going up). Those wealthy enough can fully invest in stocks as losing 50% of their portfolio doesn't alter their lifestyle. Most business owners should invest in stocks and other vehicles instead of plowing back to their businesses in order to diversify their investments.

Portfolios with more than a billion dollars such as in most mutual funds owning 10 stocks with 100 million each are just too risky to me.

Holding cash is safe but it loses its value due to inflation. To illustrate this point, consider these three scenarios in 1950:

1. An apartment bought in for $10,000 in NYC or in your home town.
2. An investment in the Dow Jones 30 Industrials for $10,000.
3. A 3.5% certificate of deposit or one of the U.S. Treasuries for your $10,000.

By now, all real estate investments should have appreciated many, many times over and most stock shares value would have multiplied also. The $10,000 CD gain has lost real value due to inflation. Our capitalist system punishes us for not taking risk. In the long term, risk is smoothed out over time.

- Excessive frequency in re-balancing your portfolio for diversification takes up time from evaluating stocks. It may cost you in transaction fees but they are low in today's self-directed brokerage accounts. In addition, it may have some tax consequences in taxable accounts.

The advantage of churning the portfolio (but not excessively) can improve the quality of your portfolio with most updated information about the companies you invest in.

Many brokers display your current diversification in your monthly statement summaries. If not, use a simple spreadsheet to classify the sectors and the asset classes in your portfolio.

- Diversification can easily be achieved by buying indexed funds and/or ETFs. They are less volatile. I recommend it to all folks with less than $50,000 to invest.
- Diversification does not mean to pick simply a stock in other sectors that has the opposite correlation from the stocks you own. The stock quality comes first.
- Diversification takes a back seat to spotting market plunges. When most stocks plunge such as during 2007-2008, diversification does not save your portfolio, but spotting and reacting to market plunges will.
- Some of our stocks will lose value. If they were due to our mistakes, write them down and learn from them. If they were frauds (not avoidable in many cases), diversification would limit our losses
- Over diversified is not too good either. With too many stocks you own, you may not have time to monitor them. Focus investing could be very profitable.

My suggestions on diversification

Portfolio up to	Strategy	For stock pickers
$ 50,000	ETF that simulates the market	5 stocks
$100,000	80% in ETF and 20% in a sector ETF(s)	10 stocks
$500,000	10 stocks with less than 3 in same sector.	15 stocks with less than 3 in same sector.
$1 Million	15 stocks + at least 20% in ETFs.	20 or more stocks depending on your time available and less than 4 in same sector.

As described, everyone's situation is different. If you have more time for investing, you should be able to handle more than 10 stocks. Playing market timing (i.e. switching to cash) depends on one's risk tolerance. If you are good at stock picking, you should buy stocks instead of ETFs. On a personal note, I usually have more than 10 stocks.

Section IV: Market Timing

1 Market timing example

The market is making new highs. There are always two camps of market timers. One camp predicts a crash is coming while the other predicts it will continue making new highs. This article includes both arguments and suggests how and what actions you need to take to protect your investments.

Management summary

The market is fundamentally unsound evidenced by fundamental metrics but technically sound evidenced by technical metrics that both will be described in this article. The data were obtained on 09/22/2018. The market has not changed a lot as of 01/2020.

Suggested actions
No one predicts the market correctly and consistently. Otherwise there are no poor folks. Moving the risky investments such as most stocks to cash too early would miss the potential profits. Moving it too late would risk the loss of your stocks.

Your actions depend on your risk tolerance. If you are conservative such as a retiree, you may want to have a larger portion of your investments in lower risk such as CDs and bonds. You can take one of the following three actions or combine all of the three actions.

1. When the market turns to technically unsound, it is time to move your stocks to cash. The market timing indicators may give false signals. In this case, the indicator would tell you to move back to stocks. Most likely you do not lose much except dealing with the consequences of taxes in non-retirement accounts.
2. Move a portion of your risky investments into cash, laddered CDs and/or short-term bonds. Again, the size of the portion depends on your risk tolerance.
3. Use stops. The sell orders would be changed to market orders when the stocks dip below prices specified by you. I prefer to use SPY or other ETF to determine the market direction. Some sectors and some stocks move faster than others. In one crash, my energy stocks were still profitable while the market was

tanking. Eventually these energy stocks caught up and fell fast. Today's highly profitable stocks are FAANG stocks as a group.

I propose and prefer 'manual stop orders' to prevent market manipulation. However, usually large ETFs cannot be manipulated easily. Manipulators try to profit from your stop orders. Set a stop order price in your `mind. When the stock falls to that specified price, sell it via a market order.

My friend confirmed my "manual stop order":

"High-frequency trading via Algo Trading Strategy can see exactly where pre-set trailing stops are and sweep across them (play them) like strings on a violin. Pre-set a trailing stop and it is bound to be triggered because Algo hunt them down. Then watch the market rip higher."

Analysis: Fundamentals and Technical

It consists of Fundamental Analysis and Technical Analysis. The former measures how expensive the current market is and the latter measures the trend of the market.

Many metrics were obtained from Finviz.com as of 9/22/2018 while others are obtained from other websites. With the exception of Fidelity.com, all websites described here are free and readily available. It also serves as a guide on how you can do your own market timing especially after a few months.

The following chart uses SPY to represent the market of the top 500 stocks. It is market cap weighted. It means the higher the market cap the stock, the higher percent of the stock is represented in the index. It turns out most are riskier FAANG stocks.

Enter Finviz.com in your browser and enter SPY. I am not responsible for any errors.

Indicator	Pass	Current Value	Indicating
• Technical			
Death Cross[1]		SMA-50 = 2.3% & SMA-200 = 6.3%	Pass
Technical Analysis: 350 SMA%[2]	>0	Price above the SMA-350.	Pass
RSI(14)	<70	61	Pass

Duration (yr.)	<5	10	Fail
		Overall	**Pass**
• Fundamental			
Valuation			
P/E[3]	<15.7	25.4	High by 62%. Fail.
Shiller P/E[3]	<16.6	33.5	High by 102%. Fail
P/B[3]	<2.78	3.52	High by 27%. Fail.
P/S[3]	<1.50	2.33	High by 55%. Fail.
Oil price	30-100	70.71	Pass
Interest rate[6] T-Bill 1 months[7]	<5	2.05	Pass
T-Bill 3 months[7]	Yield	2.18	
T-Bill 30 years[7]	Curve	3.20	Pass
Flow to Equity[4]		-3.371M	Fail
Flow to bond[4]		7.206M	
Corporate debt/GDP[8]	<40	45%	High by 13%. Fail.
USD[5]		Strong	Fail
Gold		High	Fail
Bubble		Several	Fail
Market experts		Fear long term	Neutral
Politics		Trump	Fail
Misc.		Trade war	Fail
		Overall	**Fail**

[1] This is the market timing technique without using a chart.

[2] I tried to use SMA-400% to reduce false signals without success.

[3] Get it from http://www.multpl.com/ Same as CAPE.

[4] Get it from https://www.ici.org/research/stats. It is based on 09-12-18. "Flow to Equity" is based on domestic ETF estimate. Treat it as two phases in moving to equity. First phase of moving excessively to equity indicates the market is peaking. The second phase indicates the market is plunging when flow of equity is excessively negative.

[5] Global corporations will suffer in profits converted back to USD and hard to sell to foreign countries. [4] Get it from the above link.

[6] Rising interest is bad for corporations and high-ticket products, but good for lenders.

[7] Get it from

https://www.treasury.gov/resource-center/data-chart-center/interest-rates/Pages/TextView.aspx?data=yield based on 09/21/18

[8] With the low interest rate, it may not be that critical. Corporations take advantage of the low interest rate.

Overall

Overall, technical is fine as the market is making new highs. Many aggressive investors exit the market on technical indicators only as the over-valued market could linger on for a long term such as from 2009 to 2017 so far.

Overall, fundamental is not sound. The increasing market price also is decreasing the fundamental metrics such as P/E, P/B and P/S. It is bad unless there is reason to support such as the fast earnings growth in 2009.

Many metrics are deteriorating

RSI(14) is getting closer to 65 (a passing grade specified by me).

Inverse yield curve (1.5 vs. 2.33) is about 61% apart from my interpretation and calculation. It is not a warning now but we should keep an eye on it. Most market crashes have occurred when it is 0% or negative. The theory is that in a normal case the short-term interest rates should be lower than the long-term interest rate.

Another source calculates it is 1.1% and that is very close to inversion since the last recession. From MarketWatch, the 30-year fixed interest rates is 4.66% and 1-year rate is 3.96% giving an inverse yield curve 18% apart, which is quite alarming.

Mathematically incorrect, today's full employment is at 4%. Most recessions are closely preceded by troughs in unemployment and the reverse for economy recovery.

GDP growth has been predicted from 1.8% to 3%. The 3% is from the White House for their obvious purpose. I predict it will pop up due to meeting the tariff deadlines, tax cuts and spending increases. It will then be declining to 2%. A healthy US economy should maintain 3% without special factors such as excessive immigration.

We have record debts: investors' margin, corporate debt and Federal debt. These are bubbles going to burst. Federal debt / GDP is about 95% (https://fred.stlouisfed.org/series/gfdegdq188S) today. It does not predict the market performance as this ratio was 53% and 55% before the last two market crashes. It will affect the long-term performance of the economy when we have to service the huge national debt.

We do have 10 years of stock growth at the expense of record Federal deficit. Thanks to President Obama from investors and no thanks from next generations who have to pay back our national debt. It is overdue for a correction. Hopefully it is not a crash which has an average loss of about 45%. We did have two recent corrections losing more than 10%: 2011-12 EU debt crisis and 2014-16 oil crash. The oil price has been rising from $30 per barrel to today's $70. It is still a long way from my warning of $120.

Potential triggers
Trade wars with China, Canada or EU will be the strongest trigger. Our most profitable companies are virtually all international companies. They need fair trade to prosper.

The other trigger is the possible impeachment of President Trump.

Check the validity of our charts
It seems some metrics vary. It could use after hour trading. It could be the "Days" may be "Sessions" – calendar day is different from trading session. I selected 10 years for most of the charts and StockCharts let me select only 5 years.

Here is a list of sites for charts.
https://www.stocktrader.com/2013/12/10/best-free-stock-chart-websites/
These are the three sites I use a lot: Fidelity (customers only), StockCharts and Finviz.com (missing some metrics).

As stated before, SPY may not be the best to represent the market. I prefer an ETF for 1,000 stocks and weigh the stocks evenly (i.e. not according to the market cap). Google "market timing 2020 (or current year)" for more expert info. Here is one.

Mid-year (6/15/2020) update

This is an update to my two articles: "Market timing example" and "Disaster of 2020".

Basically nothing significant has changed recently: The market is fundamentally unsound and technically sound after the recent rally. The only update is our national debt is skyrocketing. Today's "Debt/GDP" is similar to the market height in 2000 and we know what happened afterwards. That's why Buffett has accumulated a lot of cash now.

Even with the unlimited QE (i.e. printing money excessively), the high inflation and market crash predicted by many experts have not been materialized so far. This is my third prediction in "Disaster of 2020". The status of USD as a reserve currency will be shaken; I do not know when, as I do not have a time machine.

Why the market keeps going up while the economy is going down? The Fed has provided a lot of cash and the cash is chasing a fixed number of assets such as gold and stocks. It is the simple, proven theory of demand and supply. It will continue for a while as long as there is unlimited supply of money. At some point, it will pop. At that time, it could lead to a long recession, unless the economy improves as it did in 2009. The smart Fed chairman knows how it will harm the country by excessively printing money. However, he has to obey his boss who is seeking for reelection.

I expect we are in a prolonged period of low interest rates and even negative interest rates. When the rates are negative, our Treasury bonds are no longer marketable. The foreign central banks including China would dump our national debts if it has not been already started. The economy is dressed up nicely in an election year. Giving us free money is the easy way to buy votes, but the long-term effects are very harmful.

Using cheap money to buy back the company's stock would boost the stock price and hence make the management wealthier. It is a false sense of the stock value. When the company cannot pay back the debt obligations, the company would go bankrupted. If the U.S. were a company, she has gone bankrupted already.

As of 6/15/2020, QQQ (representing NASDAQ stocks) has been up 11% YTD and it is far better than DIA (representing DOW stocks) and SPY (representing the 500 large stocks in the S&P Index and losing about 5% YTD). QQQ has a lot of tech stocks while DIA has a lot of losers including Boeing. Most FAANG stocks are making record highs and QQQ is market cap weighed.

Most of the ETFs on chips have been up more than 40% in a year. I bought Amazon and two chip ETFs. I use trailing stops to protect my portfolio. Huawei is buying a lot of U.S. chips in the 120-day relaxed period. In September this year and if there is no extension, I would sell these chip ETFs fast.

I have used the strategy described in my book "Profit from the recovery of the pandemic" to take advantage of this volatile market. I used 5% as the threshold and I had too few trades; now I changed to 3%. Expecting a market crash, I weigh more on contra ETFs. As described in the same book, I bought a lot of contra ETFs, GLD and the stock of a gold miner. It is for insurance. ETFs on oil is my big mistake.

If the U.S.D. loses the status of reserve currency (not likely soon), it would bring prolonged depression and high inflation in the U.S. In this case, it is safer to invest in real estate, precious metals and profitable companies than in CDs and bonds that would lose values due to inflation.

Check out many articles on the status of the current market. Many have opposing views, so you have to make your own decision. In any case, play it safe with stops. Here is one article from MarketWatch.com.

Canary warning?

When I was working on my new book "Best stocks to buy for 2021" on Dec. 10, 2020, I found something really strange. I have never rejected so many stocks that have Fidelity's Equity Summary Score higher than 9. I rejected them as there were a lot of dumping from the insiders. Insiders know their companies better than most of us. Is it the canary telling us the market is over-valued?

Initially the following stocks have been screened by my value screens. Buy any one of the following stocks, **only** if you have good reason(s).

Symbol	Fidelity Score	Insider Purchase
BCC	9.9	-24%
GPI	10.0	-17%
HEAR	10.0	-75%
HIBB	9.4	-30%
HVT	9.5	-37%
HZO	9.5	-27%

How can HEAR score a perfect 10 while the Insiders' Transaction is -75% (I treated -2% is normal). The analysts must be wrong this time, or they believe the market will continuously make new heights. Will update the performance results later to see who is wrong.

A correction or a crash

In Dec., 2018, the S&P500 is about 15% down and a crash is about 45% down.

If a crash is coming, there should be additional 30% down. If it is a correction (15% average), then we have it already. Should we pick up bargains now? Or, are they bargains? It is a trillion dollar question.

We need a trigger for a market crash like the financial crisis in 2008 and the internet bubble in 2000. Besides the record-high margin debt, the possibility of Trump's impeachment and a trade war, I do not see any.

Filler: CIA mistook it as a missile silo in China.

2   The power of market timing

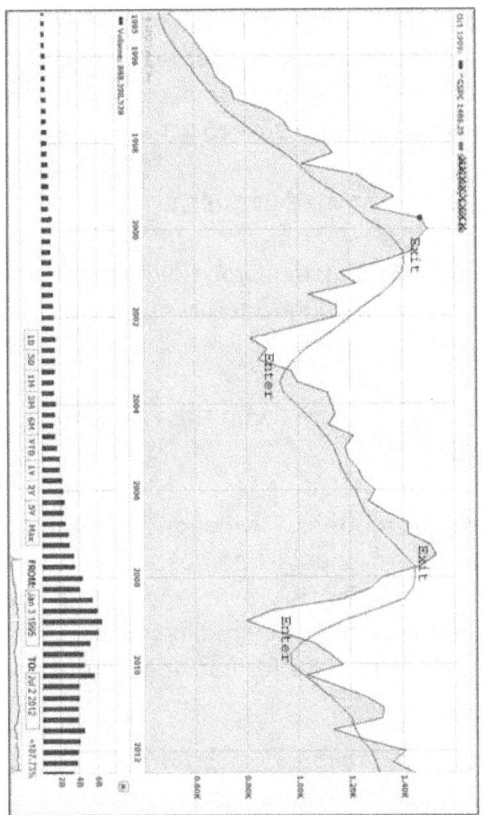

Most e-book readers allow you to select the graph to make it fit entirely on your screen. I use SPY, an ETF simulating the market. Detecting market plunges as seen in this graph indicates the exit points and reentry points also from 2000 to 9-2009 as follows.

Market Plunge	Peak	Bottom	Indicator Exit	Indicator Reenter
2000	08/28/00	09/20/02	10/01/00	06/01/03
2007	10/12/07	03/06/09	02/01/08	09/01/09
			08/01/11	11/01/11

Table: Vital Dates

For simplicity I skipped a few brief exits and reentries since 2011. You can run the simple chart once a month. When it indicates a potential market plunge is close, run the chart once a week. The last row represents a false signal.

This is based on stock prices so it may not identify the peaks and bottoms precisely, but so far it has not failed to avoid big losses and ensure big gains by reentering the market. I hope the next market plunge would give us enough time to act as these two did.

Unbelievable return with market timing

Calculate how much you made if you followed the above exit points and reenter points from 2000 to today. I bet you would have made a good fortune.

I compared the above returns with the SPY without market timing from 1-2000 to 9-2013.

There are many assumptions. Dividends and compounding are not considered. My return should be substantially better if I include buying contra ETFs during the exits and selling them during the reentries. I was shocked by the incredible return by using this simple market timing. Again, past performance does not guarantee future performances.

Summary info:

S&P 500 1-2000 to 9-2013	With Market Timing	Without Market Timing
Better	500%	
Gain	1,000	167
Gain %	68%	11%
Annualized gained	5%	1%
Days	4,959	4,959

Calculations:

S & P 500	With Market Timing	Without Market Timing
1-2000	1,469[1]	1,469[1]
Exit 10/01/00	1,041[2]	1,041
Enter 06/01/03	1,041	964[4]
Exit 02/01/08	1,489[3]	1,379[4]
Enter 09/01/09	1489	1,020[5]
Exit 08/01/11	1,888	1,293
Enter 11/01/11	1,888	1,251
09/03/13	2,469	1.638
Gained	2,469 – 1,469=1,000	1,638-1,469=167

Gain %	1000/1469 = 68%	167/1469 = 11%
Annualized gained	68% * 365/4959=5%	11%*365/4959=1%
Better	(1,000-167)/167 = 500%	

Portfolio with Market Timing:

[1] Both start with S&P 500 of 1,469 on 1-3-2000.

[2] 10/01/00
The market timing portfolio exits the market and remains the same value of 1,041 until 6/1/00.

[3] 02/01/08
The market timing portfolio exits the market and remains the same value of 1,489 until 9/1/09.

'1,489' is calculated as follows:
1,041 * (1 + Rate) = 1,041 * (1 + 1,379-964)/964) = 1,489
where the S&P 500 is 964 on 6/1/00 and 1,379 on 2/1/08.

The other calculations are based on the S&P 500 at 1,020 on 9/1/9, 1,293 on 8/1/11, 1,251 on 11/1/11 and 1,636 on 9/3/13.

Portfolio without Market Timing:

[1] Both starts with the S&P 500 of 1,469 on 1-3-2000. We could use the 9/3/13 the S&P 500 value, but it would not account for some compounded interest considerations.

[4] S&P 500 is 964 on 6/1/00 and 1,379 on 2/1/08.

[5] 02/01/08. The portfolio value is calculated to be 1,020 as follows:
1,379 * (1 + Rate) = 1,379 * (1 + (1020-1379)/1379) = 1,020
where S&P 500 is 1,379 on 2/1/08 and 1,020 on 9/1/09.

The other calculations are based on the S&P 500 at 1,293 on 8/1/11, 1,251 on 11/1/11 and 1,636 on 9/3/13.

I cannot believe the shocking return with market timing. I checked my calculations and there was nothing wrong that I could find.

3   Market cycle

"Bull markets are born on pessimism, grow on skepticism, mature on optimism, and die on euphoria" - Sir John Templeton

The stock market has cycles as our practical interpretation of the above. It is about five years apart, but it fluctuates widely. I divide it into four stages: Bottom, Early Recovery, Up and Peak.

My defined four stages of a market cycle

We need to apply the right investing strategies to each of the four stages of the cycle.

- **Bottom**

  I would not invest for at least the first six months (or even a year) after the big plunge starts, which could lose over 25% in a few months. The exceptions are investing in contra ETFs and selling short for aggressive investors.

  I estimate it will take a year from the start of the plunge to the bottom, so I will normally sell stocks early in the plunge and do not buy stocks that are in the sector (sometimes sectors) that causes the bubble for about two years after the plunge.

  At the bottom, the high-yield corporate bonds (i.e. junk bonds) would prosper when the interest rates is decreasing to stimulate the economy.

  From mid-2007 to mid-2008, bonds suffered as the investors thought the sky was falling down - it was to those who lost the jobs and/or their houses. After that, some bonds especially the long-term bonds appreciated about 50% for the following year.

  The government lowered the interest rates and these bond prices with high interest rates surged. Correct timing in buying bonds could be very profitable.

  Long-term bonds have more impact by the interest rate: The lower the interest rate, the higher the bond prices of higher-yield bonds. The older bonds with higher interest rates are more valuable to the newer bonds with lower interest rates.

I define this period of the bottom from the start of the plunge to the start of Early Recovery.

- **Early Recovery**

It usually starts after one year from the plunge; no one can pin point the exact time consistently. By this time preferably earlier, we should have closed out all positions in contra ETFs and shorts.

Roughly speaking, October, 2007 (some use 2008) is the start of the market plunge. March, 2009 is the end of the bottom stage and the start of the early recovery stage of the 2007 cycle. However, every market cycle is different in where it starts and ends.

The one-year gain from the bottom is most profitable. It usually gains over 25% in a year from the market bottom. I, a conservative investor, had huge gains using some leverage in my largest taxable account in 2009. From my memory, I had a similar return in 2003 but I had not saved the statement as in 2009.

In this phase, value is a better parameter than growth in searching for stocks. If your investment subscription provides a composite value score and a composite timing score, the sort parameter of your screened stocks could be "Composite Value / Composite Timing" in descending order. Select the top stocks in this order. You still have to analyze the top-screened stocks.

Forward (same as Expected) P/E is a good metric. However, most companies may be losing money at this stage. Those companies that can last for more than one year with its cash reserve are potential good buys. The best appreciated stocks are beaten companies that have precious technologies and good customer bases. They could be candidates to be acquired if they are small enough.

- **Up**

  Usually the growth metrics such as <u>PEG</u> could be better than the value metrics such as expected P/E during this phase. Most stocks are winners except contra ETFs and shorting stocks. When the growth stocks are making headlines and the defensive stocks are being dumped, this is the hint that we're well into the Up phase of the market cycle.

  Locate stocks with growth metrics such as favorable PEG and high SMA-200% (from Finviz.com). Do not be scared on how much they have already appreciated. The strategy "Buy High and Sell Higher" works in this phase. Protect your profits with stops.

  Ensure that they have value too. Skip the stocks with expected P/Es higher than 35 unless there are good reasons. Most stocks will gain due to the tide of the market. However, when they're overbought (RSI(14) over 60), be careful. When institutional investors sell these stocks, they will crash.

- **Peak**

  When everyone makes easy money and the interest rates is high, watch out. Stop loss and/or stop limit should be used to protect your investment. Check out whether there is any bubble that would be burst like the internet in 2000 and the finance (and housing) in 2007.

  Internet crisis is easy to spot, but not the financial crisis. In 2007 we had a cycle longer than the average which is about 5 years. The plunge is very fast and very steep – thanks to the institutional investors who drive the market down.

  Run the technical analysis chart described in the Chapter on Spotting Big Market Plunges at least monthly (weekly if you have time). Protect your investment. Do not fall in love with any stock (you can buy it back later at a deep discount). Making the last buck is a fool's game.

Accumulate cash according to your risk tolerance. A retiree or a conservative investor would accumulate from 25% to 50% and should be ready to move to all cash when the plunge starts.

We can lower the cash percent if we use enough stop loss protection. Be psychologically prepared because the stock market may still rise for a while. There is no perfect market timing.

The 2007 Cycle

The market plunged starting in 10-2007 and ending in 3-2009 (bottom), started to recover in 3-2009 (early recover), and trended up from 2010 to 1-2013 (the up phase of the market cycle). As of 3/2016, it is the peak phase defined by me.

As of 1/2013, we have recovered all the market losses since 2007. However, as of 7/2014, the economy has not fully recovered compared to the economy before the plunge. The employment judging by the medium salary has not fully recovered and the economy is not expanding. It is uncommon that the economy does not follow the market. It is due to the excessive supply of money by the government and partly due to globalization to allow companies to hire overseas.

Although a W-shaped recession seldom happens, we have a chance today. We hope we do not have a depression and/or the similar lost decades that Japan has been experiencing. Some may conclude we are close to completing a market cycle from 2007 to 2016. As of 2016, the economy is recovering slowly and we're better than most other global economies.

Again, market timing is not an exact science as it involves irrational human beings and government interventions. The timing using market cycle described here is a guideline as it is hard to time it exactly.

The average market cycle is about 5 years, but they fluctuate. If we consider 2007 as the plunge, we have about 8 years of this cycle as of 2015.

In a typical cycle (few are typical), we have about one year in each of the 4 phases I defined (plunge, early recovery, up and peak).

Events/Triggers

There are financial events and triggers that cause the transition of one phase of the market cycle to another. They usually do not change the sequence of the phases (say not from Peak to Early Recovery), but they may change the duration of the phase. Examples are:

- The government announcing change of the interest rate,
- Change of employment, and
- Change of GNP.

Sectors in a market cycle (my suggestion)

Market Phase	Favorable		Unfavorable
Early Recovery	Financial, Technology, Industrial		Energy, Telecom, Utilities
Up	Technology, Industrial, Housing		
Peak	Mineral, Health Care, Energy, Long-Term Bond, Consumer Discretionary		
Bottom	Consumer Staples, Utilities		Consumer Discretionary, Technology, Industrial, Long-Term & high-yield Bond

The sectors that cause the recession usually take a longer time to recover. In 2000, the technology sector was not favorable in the Early Recovery phase, contrary to the above table. In 2007, the financial sector was not favorable in the Early Recovery phase. These are the "offending" sectors that cause the plunges.

In a recession, we usually cannot cut down on consumer staples and utilities, but we can cut down on buying consumer gadgets. Companies usually postpone investing in equipment and systems during a recession and expand when the economy is humming. The government usually lowers the interest rates right after the plunge to stimulate the economy.

Conclusion

When the market is about to plunge or change from one stage to another, run the described chart more frequently and read more articles written by the experts.

Again, market timing is not an exact science but it is based on educated guesses. The better guesses should have more rights than wrongs in the long term. Our actions depend on our risk tolerance. Be careful on using any new strategy that has not been fully understood and proven. Since 2000, market timing is very important to your financial health with two market plunges with an average of about 45% loss.

4 Calendar Timing table

I made the following charts so it is easier to time the market by calendar.

All dates are inclusive.

No.	Metric		Score
1	Seasonal	Nov. - April, Score = 1	
2	Best Month	Nov., Score = 1	
		Sep., Score = -1	
3	Best Days	Dec. 15 – Jan.15 Score = 1	
4	Presidential Cycle	Election Year, Score = 1	
		1st Year in Office, Score = -1	
		2nd year, Score = -1	
		3rd year, Score = 2	
5	Presidential[3]	Democratic = 1 Republican = -1	
6	Market Cycle	Early Recovery, Score = 3	
		Up, Score = 2	
		Peak, Score = 1	
7	SPY (Finviz.com)	SMA200% > 8%[2] Score = -1	
		SMA200% < 0 Score = -1	
		RSI(14) > 65% Score = -1	
		Grand Score	

Footnote.
1   Refer to Market Cycle chapter on how I define phases of a cycle.
2   For simplicity, use Finviz.com. Enter SPY and you will find SMA200% and RSI(14) to predict whether the market is peaking and overbought.
3   I'm political neutral. The selection is based on historical statistics.

Add up all the scores. The passing grade is 0. According to my table which is based on my personal selections/preferences, the market is favorable when the grand score is 1 or higher. I bet it is the first time you see such a scoring system for market timing.

Sectors for market cycle

Market Phase[1]	Favorable		Unfavorable
Early Recovery	Financial, Technology, Industrial		Energy, Telecom, Utilities
Up	Technology, Industrial		
Peak	Mineral, Health Care, Energy		
Bottom	Consumer Staples, Utilities		Consumer Discretionary, Technology, Industrial
Seasonal	**Favorable**		**Unfavorable**
Winter	Energy, Utilities		
End of year	QQQ, EWG		
Olympics	ETF for host country[2]		

Footnote.
1   Refer to Market Cycle chapter on how I define phases of a cycle.
2   Buy it next year after Olympics. It could be due to higher GDP or the publicity. However, be selective. Greece is too small a country to host an Olympics.

5   Six signs of a correction

The following is an article titled "Six signs of a correction" I wrote for Seeking Alpha on June 29, 2014.

http://seekingalpha.com/article/2291605-6-signs-of-a-correction?v=1404308839

The best protection is playing defense now. The chance of a correction (10% or more) is high.

Six signs of a correction

1. All my technical indicators show the market is peaking and overbought. SPY is an ETF simulating the market of the S&P 500 stocks. As of 6/29/2014, the RSI(14) is at 67% and the SMA-200% is at 8.35%. SMA-200% measures how far away the stock price is from its simple moving average of the last 200 trade sessions.

    You may argue that you do not believe in technical analysis. However, many institutional fund managers learn technical analysis and they will act accordingly. It is one of the many tools that hedge fund managers use to 'hedge'. Most mutual fund managers cannot practice market timing bound by the rules and regulations.

2. Newton's Law of Gravity has never been proven wrong (some humor to get your attention). What goes up must come down. The market has been up even after inflation. However, it takes a breather from time to time. A small one is called a correction and a big one is called a market plunge.

3. We did not have one such correction of 10% in 2013, so the time is ripe. The average is about one correction of 10% or more and about 1.5 corrections for 5% in a year. Many experts predicted wrongly on a correction in 2013. I do not bet against them to be wrong two times in a row.

4. There are more articles predicting a correction than articles arguing against it. It could be a self-fulfilling prophesy. It is the herd psychology. One's opinion.

5. The market has low volumes and narrow ranges for many days may indicate that the market is changing direction. The sea is calmest before a storm.
6. I am not convinced that I can make a lot of profit even if there is no correction. To me, the market is fully valued. It is my reward / risk ratio. I prefer not to make the last buck and have a good sleep.

How to protect yourself

It depends on your risk tolerance.

1. Accumulate cash from 0% to 50%. I recommend 15% for most. 0% is for those who ignore the signs. It was a great selection for 2013. I select 50% as I'm more conservative than most.
2. Place stop orders. Adjust them when they appreciate. Some stocks are more volatile than others. I prefer to use stop orders in market plunges rather than corrections, as corrections are too brief to be effective.
3. Short the market. I do not recommend shorting in most cases. Buying a contra ETF may help. In any case, do not risk money you cannot afford to lose.
4. Use options to protect your portfolio.
5. Prepare a list of stocks to buy when there is a correction, and wait for better time to invest.

Do not treat my (or all others') predictions as gospel. Predictions are just predictions. It is like buying insurance that we do not expect to collect from.

I have to admit market timing is not an exact science. Hopefully we are more right than wrong.

Summary of comments on the article

There are two camps: one who believe and one who do not believe. It is as expected. I will not take credit if there will be a correction within a month, or take the blame if there will be none in the next 3 months. From my record, I have more right than wrong predictions, but it may have nothing to do with future market predictions. Here is my summary:

1. I did think of other signs as mentioned by some of my readers: interest rate, oil price, current events... I expect interest rates will start rising by the end of the year. The recent rise in oil price is due to the turmoil in the Middle East. The current events including Ukraine and the Middle East seem not to be a factor as our leader does not want to participate in this.

2. I do not expect a market plunge (over 30% down) as I do not see any bubbles (those bubble stocks are too few). My prediction: These bubble stocks will be half the peaks achieved in 2013 and 2014 by the end of 2014. To me, all stock trades are predictions. Some materialize and some do not.

3. Corrections are harder to detect than market plunges. After I detect a plunge, I will spend most of my time in protecting my portfolio.

##Fillers:

Where common sense is not common sense

Excessive printing of money is not a long-term solution. Servicing the huge debt weakens our competitiveness. The politicians just want to buy votes today and finance their campaigns. Our next generations will have to pay for these huge debts.

I have never taken any business classes unless required for my engineering degrees and yet I can understand it via common sense. I wonder why our highly-educated (at least by their Ph.D. certificates), smartly-looking (looks could be deceiving), high salaried (many times higher than mine) decision makers do not understand and act on it.

On Shooting and any violence. "Forgive" is the most powerful word in any language in any culture. "Pray for the victims" do not do any good, but take actions to prevent similar shootings from happening. PLEASE.

6 Technical analysis (TA)

The basics

Technical analysis (a.k.a. charting) is easier to learn than you might expect. It represents the trend of the market (a stock or a group of stocks) graphically. If more investors are in the market, the market would move upwards until it changes direction. We divide the trends into short-term, intermediate-term and long-term.

The chartists usually do not consider fundamentals as they believe they have already been priced into the stock price and some fundamentals are not available to the public. To illustrate, a new drug has been discovered, the stock price of the company jumps initially by insiders purchases and the informed. Its fundamental metrics do not demonstrate this right away, but many investors are buying to boost up the stock price as evidenced by the technical indicators such as SMA for 20 or 50 days.

The volume is a confirmation. When the stock moves up or down by 10% with a low volume, the trend is not yet confirmed.

The trend of the stock price is not a straight line in most cases. Hence a trend line is usually drawn to indicate the direction of the stock. Many investors believe the stocks fluctuate in certain ranges (i.e. channels) and the chart draws the upper value (the resistance line) and the lower value (the support line). In theory, the price of a stock fluctuates within the resistance line (ceiling for understanding) and support (floor). When it reaches its support, it becomes a buy and vice versa for a sell. Most charts including Finviz.com would display these lines.

When the price passes out of the channel, it is called a breakout. Darvas, one of the oldest and most successful chartists, profited from the breakouts of the resistance line and believed the stock was close to the support line of the new channel. Hence it would be a long way up in theory.

If it were so simple, there will be no poor folks

It works most of the time, but do not place all your money on it. For chartists, 51% is great (the same for playing Black Jack). Some trends reverse very fast such as the bio drug stocks in 2015. You need to hedge your bets such as placing stop orders. Most do not want to spend their lives in watching the trend from a big screen.

Most novices use too many technical indicators and lose in their performances to the professionals. Recently, most chartists were not doing all that great and I did not find many books on their success than a decade ago. It could be due to too many followers in similar setups. I verified it with my recent testing using Finviz.com.

Simple Moving Average

The basic technical indicator is SMA-N. It is the average of the last N trade sessions. When N is 20 (or SMA-20), we classify it as short-term. Similarly, SMA-50 is an intermediate-term and SMA-200 is long-term. I prefer 50, 100 and 250. This trend duration is important. For example, do not want to place long-term purchases using the short-term SMA-50. There are many modifications to SMA such as giving more weight to recent data, but I have not found them any better. Finviz.com includes this information without charting (SMA-20, SMA-50 and SMA-100 in percentages).

Defining the trend periods is rather arbitrary. I use SMA-350 to detect the market plunges and SMA-100 for stocks. Weighted Moving Average weighs more weight on recent price data.

It can be used to determine whether we are in bull, bear or a sideways market using SMA-50 (or SMA-200 for longer term) for the market (using SPY), the sector (using an ETF for the sector and the specific stock. The trend is up when it the price is above the SMA and the reversal of the trend.

https://www.youtube.com/watch?v=jdYNaE5GJ0k&list=WL&index=5&t=609s

The trend is your best friend
Most traders use TA for trending in a short duration. Investors can also use TA to time the entry and exit points for better potential

profits. Value investors usually are patient and they do bottom fishing and they search for 'oversold' condition using RSI(14). Again high volume is a confirmation.

Many sites provide charting free of charge such as Yahoo!Finance. Finviz.com provides a lot of technical indicators without charting such as SMA% and RSI(14). It also provides screen searching for stocks that meet your technical analysis criteria.

Hands on
Bring up Finviz.com and enter any stock symbol such as AAPL. You can see the daily prices of AAPL from about nine months ago to today. Three SMAs (Simple Moving Average) are displayed as SMA-20, SMA-50 and SMA-200. The first two are for short-term trends. When the price is above the SMA, it is expected to be trending up. Again, the trade volume is used as a confirmation.

You can also see the resistance line and the support line drawn. In theory, the stock will trade within these lines. When it exceeds its resistance line, it is called a breakout, and vice versa for a breakdown. Sometimes it displays some technical patterns such as Cup and Shoulder and Double Down (both are positive patterns).

Select Weekly data. The Candle chart is better described than the Daily chart. Candles give us better descriptions of the price: open, close, high and low. The green color indicates the price is up for the period (a week in this example) and the red color indicates a down period.

In addition, Finviz.com includes some technical indicators in the metric section such as RSI. Most other chart sites are similar in the basics. Use Finviz's Help and select Technical Analysis for more description. Investopedia has enhanced descriptions on this topic.

TA patterns

There are many TA patterns such as Bollinger Bands and MACD. The patterns are based on the stock prices and many times they prove to be correct predictions especially on stocks with high volume and high market caps. Patterns have been repeating themselves many times as they are driven by investors.

Sites for TA

There are many free sites for charts with explanations of their technical indicators. Popular ones include BigCharts.com, SmallCharts.com and Yahoo!Finance. Fidelity includes some unique features in its charts such as P/E.

Why I do not use TA as a primary tool for stock picking

My investing style is different from a day trader's. I prefer to 'Buy Low and Sell High' instead of 'Buy High and Sell Higher'. I try to find the real bottom price. TA will not find the bottom very easily but it tracks the trend better. As a bargain hunter, I do not expect the stock will rise fast as I'm usually swimming against the tide. However, value stocks could stay in the low price for a long time (i.e. value trap). I like to select stocks that turn around as evidenced by the SMA-20 and SMA-50.

With that said, my momentum portfolio has appreciated consistently and usually has the best performing stocks among all my portfolios. It is based on the timely grade from my subscriptions plus the metrics on timing.

Most chartists would also tell you to buy the stocks that have broken out (i.e. higher than the resistance line) and/or stocks at their highs. Contrary to value investing, you should exit when the trend reverses. The reversal could happen very fast and hence protect your portfolio by setting up stop loss (preferably with trailing stop) orders.

My opinion

I do not want to argue whether TA is good for you or not. You need to find that out. Most likely, the day traders and very short-term traders will profit more from TA than the investors seeking value stocks for the long-term gains.

7 Disrupting innovation

New technologies may change our lives. It would profit our prosperity by investing in the right companies that would profit from these technologies and divesting from the companies that these technologies would harm them.

There have been many disruptive technologies in the past. Roughly I divided into the following phases in our recent history: Phase 1 (electricity and steam engine), Phase 2 (computer), Phase 3 (internet) and today's Phase 4.

Many technologies converge or are implemented in one sector such as 5G and battery technology into self-driving cars. With the exceptions of 5G and Blockchain that are too wide a topic to summarize here, the following will be described briefly and several links are available to further your research. Some are materializing today in 2020 and they should affect us for the coming decade. Most are fundamentally unsound by our metrics.

- Electric cars. Eventually they will outsold combustion cars. Companies: Tesla and battery research companies. Badly affected companies: auto companies that do not adapt and oil.
- Energy renewable technology. Eventually, cost per energy unit would favor them compared to oil.
- Robots would affect jobs.
- Fintech. Almost all Chinese consumers are using phone as the wallet and it will not be too long for U.S. to accept mobile payment. Companies: Paypal and Square. Retails and restaurants could harm their profits in 2020. Badly affected companies: banks that do not adapt.
- Cryptocurrency. Eventually there will be less than 5 and most are issued by bank and country with good record.
- Gene modifying companies. It has fixed many and continues to fix many diseases by re-programing bad genes. Companies: CRIPR. Badly affected companies: drug companies that do not co-operate with CRISPR, Editas Medicine and Intellia Therapeutics.
- AI, artificial intelligence. We have good research but our privacy restriction limits our implementation. Companies: many Chinese companies in this sector.

Bonus - Define Insider Trading

Investopedia defines it as:

"Insider trading can be illegal or legal depending on when the insider makes the trade: it is illegal when the material information is still nonpublic--trading while having special knowledge is unfair to other investors who don't have access to such knowledge. Illegal insider trading therefore includes tipping others when you have any sort of nonpublic information. Directors are not the only ones who have the potential to be convicted of insider trading. People such as brokers and even family members can be guilty.

Insider trading is legal once the material information has been made public, at which time the insider has no direct advantage over other investors. The SEC, however, still requires all insiders to report all their transactions. So, as insiders have an insight into the workings of their company, it may be wise for an investor to look at these reports to see how insiders are legally trading their stock."

If you need more information, click this link from Wikipedia. http://en.wikipedia.org/wiki/Insider_trading

My additions to conventional insider trading

Hopefully my additions improve the performance of this strategy that has already been proven to work most of the time.

- I add market timing to Insider Trading. You need to sell most stocks except contra ETFs before a market plunge and buy them back as indicated by the chart.

- Diversify your portfolio. Keep 10 stocks for a portfolio less than a million. Ensure that there are not more than 3 stocks in the same sector. Keep 20 stocks for portfolio over a million. Too many stocks would require more of your time that would be better spent in evaluating individual stocks. Too few of stocks would impact your portfolio when one stock has a big loss.

It is just a recommendation. Vary your holding size and holding period according to your time, your portfolio size and your expertise in the sector.

- Stick with stocks over $2, average daily volume over 10,000 shares (8,000 for stock prices over $25) and market cap over 200 million.

  Most big winners usually are in the price range between the $2 and $15 price and market cap between 200 million to 800 million. They represent the stocks that big boys are ignoring due to their restrictions. This is just a general guideline and there are always exceptions. Change them according to your requirements.

  I prefer to skip stocks from most emerging countries, especially the smaller companies as I do not trust their financial statements.

- Ignore the subscription services or books claiming they are making over 30% consistently. Some even have examples of making 5,000%. Most likely they tell you the winners but not their losers. It is easy to pick up winners that fit their strategy but it does not tell you the real performance.

  Check whether their portfolio uses cash or not as it cannot be manipulated such as using the best prices of the day to trade. I bet that those portfolios consistently making over 30% are not real. Alternatively they have 10 portfolios and they only show you the one that makes a good profit.

  When they back test their strategies, they cheat their performances with survivor bias (i.e. those bankrupt stocks are not in the historical database). If their returns are that great, do you think they will share their secrets with you?

  Some made a big fortune and lost it all. So, the turtle investors who make small profits consistently and keep most of the wins fare far better than making millions in a year and losing it all in next year. Market timing and diversifying our portfolio would help us win consistently in the long run.

Bonus - A turnaround strategy

Many value stocks tend to stay in this phase for a long time. When the turnaround starts, it could be very profitable.

Market Timing

Do not buy any stock when the market is risky as described elsewhere in the book. Actually you should sell most of the stocks when the market is risky.

Buy Metrics

Metric	Value	Conservative	Aggressive
General			
Market Cap	>300 M	>1,000 M	>100 M
Price	> 2	>10	>1
Avg. Volume	>20,000	>50,000	>10,000
USA	Only	Only	Foreign but listed in USA
Fundamental			
Forward P/E	<15	<10	<25
Earning Gr Q-Q	>5%	>8%	>3%
ROE	>10	>15	>5
P / FCF	<10	<8	<15
Debt / Equity	<.5	<.25	<1
Technical			
SMA-50%	>10	>15	>5
Misc.			
Blue Chip Growth	A or B	A	A or B
Fidelity	>6	>8	>5
IBD	>60	>90	>50
Vector Vest	>=1	>=0.8	>=12
Value Line Proj. 3-5% return	>5%	>10%	>5%
Zacks	>=4	5	>=4
ASSS	>=2	>=5	>=2

The assignment values for the metrics are not fixed; feel free to change it according to your own risk level. I do have suggestions for conservative investors and aggressive investors.

Some of the metrics are not readily available in Finviz.com and the following describes how to modify them.

Explanation

- Market Cap. The free version of Finviz.com does not allow you to specify the range. Use 'Any' and then select the stocks according to the specified values. Average Volume has the similar restriction.
- The conservative values for Market Cap, Price and Average Volume try to select larger companies. The aggressive values try to select smaller companies, which historically are more risky but perform better.
- I prefer 'USA' for Country. Stay away from small companies from developing countries unless you can trust their financial statements.
- Forward P/E measures the value of the stock. Ensure "E" (Earnings) is positive. I prefer it over P/E (from the last twelve months).
- Earnings Growth Quarter to last Quarter is preferred to be positive unless it is during a recession.
- ROE measures how well the company has been managed.
- P/FCF. "Price / Free Cash Flow" cannot be manipulated easily. Together with low "Debt / Equity", it measures whether the company would bankrupt.
- SMA-50%. Some stocks tend to stay in a value stage for a long while (termed value trap). We like to select stocks just starting being noticed and on its way up.
- Misc. Many sites have evaluated the stocks for us. Some only let their customers to access such information, some are available for free trials or are available from the library.
- ASSS is my scoring system.

With the above, I have 35 stocks on 10/28/16. If you need 10 stocks for further evaluation, try to sort Forward P/E in descending order and select the top 10. If you cannot find any or substantially less than normal, it implies the market is risky, so take a break. If the performances of the last few stocks you selected are poor, take a break too as the market conditions do not favor the value metrics we specified.

Qualitative analysis

Double click on the stock and read as many articles described on the stock as possible. If it meets all the criteria, buy the stock. Recommend to use market orders for large companies in a non-volatile market (when the average daily fluctuation is less than 0.5%). If the selected stock is the one you just sold, make you only buy it after 31 days to avoid Wash Sale penalty.

Keeping informed

Check the company updates of the stock you owned every month. One easy way is to enter the stocks in a portfolio in SeekingAlpha.com.

Sell the stock

Re-evaluate the stocks every 6 months.

If it does not meet the criteria or the market is risky, sell it. If it is only a few days away from the long-term capital gain, sell the losers right away or hold on the winner for a few more days.

Re-balance the portfolio after a stock has been sold. Ensure it is diversified enough into large/small cap and sectors.

Top-down Investing

It is similar to the above. Find the sectors that perform the best last month. Under Finviz.com, select the best sector under 'sector' one at a time. Several sites such as Fidelity compare the stock to the averages of stocks in the same sector.

Appendix 1 – All my books

- Complete the Art of Investing (highly recommended combining most of my books on investing). The Kindle version has over 850 pages (6*9), about 3 times the size of an investing book.
- Sector Rotation: 21 Strategies and another book Shorting (highly recommended for short-term investors) have more specific chapters on the topic and share many articles with "Complete the art of investing".
- Best stocks for 2022 (avail after Dec. 15, 2021).
- "Nuclear War with China".
- Books for today's market: Profit from Coming Market Crash.
- The following books are in a series: Finding Profitable Stocks, Market Timing and Scoring Stocks. Alternate books: Using Fidelity and Using Finviz.
- Books on strategies: "Profit from bull, bear and sideways markets" (Rotation + Momentum + ETF Rotation + trend following), Trading System (similar to printed version of Complete), Swing (Rotation + Momentum), ETF Rotation for Couch Potatoes, Momentum, SuperStocks, Dividend, Penny & Micro Stock, and Retiree.
- Books for advance beginners: Be an expert (highly recommended), Introduce, Investing for Beginners, Beat Fund Managers, Profit via ETFs, Buffett, Ideas, Conservative and Top-Down.
- Miscellaneous: Lessons in Investing. Investing Strategies. Buy Low and Sell High. Buy High and sell Higher. Buffettology. Technical Analysis. Trading Stocks.
- Concise Editions and Introduction Editions are available at very low prices and are competitive with books of similar sizes (50 pages) and prices ($3 range).

Most books have paperbacks. Links and offers are subject to change without notice.

Best stocks to buy for 2022 (avail. after Dec. 15, 21)

We care about performance only. Not considering dividends and fees, my last three books in this series have beaten the SPY (the market to most) by **110%, 71% and 25%** from the publish date to 07/01/2021.

Book	Stocks	Return	Ann.	Beat SPY by
Best Book for 2021 2nd Edition	10	20%	52%	110%
Best Book for 2021	4	29%	52%	71%
Best Book to Buy from Aug, 2020	14	42%	45%	25%
Avg.	9	31%	50%	69%

Appendix 2 – Complete the Art of Investing

Instead of buying 16 books, why not buy one book (Complete the Art of Investing) consisting of 16 books? Besides saving money and your digital shelve space, it gives you quick reference and concentration on the topic you're currently interested in. It covers most investing topics in investing excluding speculative investing such as currency trading and day trading.

The Kindle version has about 850 pages (6*9), about the size of three books of average size. With the cost of $10 and at least 850 investing ideas, it is about one cent per idea. Most other books have only a few ideas in the entire book

The 16 books

This book "Complete Art of Investing" is divided into 16 books as follows. Click for the link to the book described in Amazon.com. I squeezed more than 3,000 pages into 850 pages by eliminating duplicated information such as evaluating stocks.

Book No.	Amazon.com
1	Simple techniques
2	Finding Stocks
3	Evaluating Stocks
4	Scoring Stocks
5	Trading Stocks
6	Market Timing
7	Strategies
8	Sector Rotation
9	Insider Trading
10	Penny Stocks & Micro Cap
11	Momentum Investing
12	Dividend Investing
13	Technical Analysis
14	Investing Ideas
15	The Economy
16	Buffettology

The book links are subject to change without notice.

"How to be a billionaire" is for beginners and couch potatoes, who can use the advanced features of this book in the simplest and less time-consuming techniques. Most advance users can skip this section unless they want to use some of the short cuts described.

We start with the basic books Finding Stocks, Evaluate Stocks, Trading Stocks and Market Timing. You can select and start with one of the many styles and strategies in investing such as swing trading and top-down strategy. Many tools are described in other books such as ETFs, technical analysis, covered calls and trading plan.

Many books start with "Why" to lure you to read more and are followed by "How" and then the theory behind the book.
If the book you're reading is beneficial to you, imagine how it would with 850 pages.

Most readers' comments are on "Debunk the Myths in Investing", which this book is originally based on. As of 2018, I did not know any of the commentators on my books.

"I skipped ahead to his chapter book 14 (of "Complete the Art of Investing"), Investment Advice just to get a feel of his writing style. His research is phenomenal and doesn't overwhelm with big words or catchy "sales-like" tactics.

I truly believe this ordinary man, Mr. Tony Pow, has a gift of explaining his experience as an investor without the bull crap of trying to make you buy his stuff. He seemingly just wants to share his knowledge, tips, and clarity of definitions for the kind of folks like me who want to understand something FIRST before jumping in with emotions of trying to make a boat load of money. I like the technical analysis side he brings.

Mr. Tony Pow talks about hidden gems in his book; well....quite frankly, he is a hidden gem. Thank you and I will also post my comments about this author to my Facebook page!" – JB on this book.

"Excellent book, recommend to all investors... great knowledge. It has fine-tuned my investing strategies... Your book is hard to set aside, as I read it all the time learning good techniques and analysis of stocks, ETF... Since I purchased your book in March, I have underlined, highlighted and placed tabs on top of pages for quick reference." – Aileron on this book.

"Tony, I just finished reading your 2nd edition. It's my pleasure to report that I found it most interesting. You're welcome to use this blurb if you like:

Debunk the Myths in Investing is an all-encompassing look at not only the most salient factors influencing markets and investors, but also a from-the-trenches look at many of the misconceptions and mistakes too many investors make. Reading this book may save not only time and aggravation but money as well!"

Joseph Shaefer, CEO, Stanford Wealth Management LLC.

"Tony, Great work!" from James and Chris, who are portfolio managers.

"'Debunk the Myths in Investing' is a comprehensive book on investing that deals with many aspects of this tense profession in which with a lot of knowledge and a bit of luck (or vice versa) one can greatly benefit...

Therefore 'Debunk the Myths in Investing' is an interesting book that on its 500 pages offer a lot of knowledge related to investing world and many practical advice, so I can recommend its reading if you're interested in this topic."
- Denis Vukosav, Top 500 Reviewers at Amazon.com.

"490 pages (Debunk) of a genius's ranting and hypothesis with various theories throughout, written light-heartedly with ample doses of humor...Yes, the myth of not being able to profitably time the market is BUSTED...

One might ask... Why is he giving away the results of his hard-earned research for only $20? He states that his children are not interested in investing and wants to share his efforts with the world." - Abe Agoda.

"Excellent book, recommend to all investors... great knowledge. It has fine-tuned my investing strategies... Your book is hard to set aside, as I read it all the time learning good techniques and analysis of stocks, ETF... Since I purchased your book in March, I have underlined, highlighted and placed tabs on top of pages for quick reference." - Aileron on this book.

"Great stuff, Tony. It's great to meet experienced traders such as yourself. I had a browse through the book and think your method is a little more refined than mine."
"Your strategy is very rules based and solid. I sometimes envy people who have developed something like this."

Making 50% in one month
I claim to have the best one-month performance ever for recommending 8 or more stocks without using options and leverage. My following return is 57% in a month or 621% annualized. They are slightly different as I calculated the average from the averages of three different accounts. The average buy date is 12/26/18 and the "current date" is 01/28/19.
The performance may not be repeated. I will use the same screen for the coming years and even the expected 10% (or 120% annualized) is very good.

I used the same screen for searching stock candidates. I spent a total of about 20 hours from Dec. 15, 2018 to Jan. 5, 2019.

Stock	Buy Price	Sold or Current Price	Buy date	Sold or Current date	Profit %	Profit % Ann.	Status
CHK	2.13	2.99	01/03/09	01/18/19	40%	982%	Sold
MNK	16.41	21.45	01/03/19	01/25/19	31%	510%	Sold
MNK	16.43	21.45	01/03/19	01/25/19	31%	507%	Sold
NNBR	5.68	8.58	12/26/18	01/28/19	51%	565%	
NNBR	5.72	8.58	12/26/18	01/28/19	66%	727%	
ESTE	4.35	6.45	12/26/18	01/18/19	48%	766%	Sold
LCI	4.61	8.29	12/21/18	01/28/19	80%	767%	
MDR	8.01	9.13	01/08/19	01/28/19	14%	255%	
YRCW	3.29	5.78	12/21/18	01/28/19	76%	727%	
YRCW	3.26	5.78	12/21/18	01/28/19	77%	742%	
ASRT	3.56	4.18	12/26/18	01/28/19	17%	193%	
UTCC	7.13	11.00	12/26/18	01/28/19	54%	600%	

YRCW	2.92	5.78	12/26/18	01/28/19	98%	1083%	

Best one-year return

I claim to have the best-performed article in Seeking Alpha history, an investing site, for recommending 15 or more stocks in one year after the publish date without using options and leverage.

https://seekingalpha.com/article/1095671-amazing-returns-velti-alcatel-lucent-alpha-natural-resources

Your choice

"Complete the art of investing" should be your first choice. If you are short-term trading, I recommend "Sector Rotation: 21 Strategies" and "Shorting Stocks /ETFs". These 3 books together with "Using Fidelity" share many articles.

My recommended stocks can be found in my "Best stocks" series. It would be published on Dec. 15 – it is not a promise. So far, this book and "Sector Rotation: 21 Strategies" are my best sellers. All info are subject to change without notice.

Sector Rotation: 21 Strategies

In addition, as of 5/2020 I bet that no author besides me made **over 4 times** using sector rotation starting the amount more than his yearly salary then.

- On 5/26/2020, I searched for "Sector Rotation" under Amazon's Book. They are listed in the same order except my book Sector Rotation: 21 Strategies.

Book	Date	Size[1]	Kindle $[1]	Hard $
Sector Rotation: 21 Strategies	**05/2020**	**425**	**$9.95**	$24.95
Super Sectors	09/2010	289	$26.39	$49.95
Dual Momentum Investing	11/2014	240	$40.40	$42.20
Sector Investing	05/1996	260		$29.94
Sector Trading Strategies	08/2007	164	$26.39	$16.66
The Sector Strategist	03/2012	225	$26.39	$44.96
ETF Rotation	10/2012	125	**$9.95**	**$14.99**

Optimal... Sector Rotation	07/2015	80		$44.07

[1] From Amazon on size and prices as of 5/25/2020. Last update is 09/2021.

My book won in all categories except the price for hard copy in one. However, my book won as the lowest cost per page by a wide margin.

- I have **21** strategies in sector rotation while most books have only one. It ranges from simple rotation of a stock ETF and cash for beginners to many advanced strategies for experts. Most other books have one or two strategies.
- Andrew, a contributor on Sector Rotation article at Seeking Alpha, said, "Great stuff, Tony. It's great to meet experienced traders such as yourself. I had a browse through the book and think your method is a little more refined than mine."
- "You have written the book in a way that makes good and logical sense." Bill.
- Do not be fooled by past performances. Just check the recent performance of the top 50 stocks selected by IBD in the last five years. The mediocre result (hopefully it will change) could be due to too many followers and/or there is no evergreen strategy.
- I switched most (if not all) of my sector funds in April, 2000 from technology sectors to traditional sectors (better to money market fund). We can reduce losses by spotting market plunges and the sector trend.

Appendix 3 - Our window to the investing world

The paperback version of this chapter can be found in the following link.
http://ebmyth.blogspot.com/2013/11/web-sites.html

- **General**
  Wikipedia / Investopedia /Yahoo!Finance / MarketWatch / Cnnfn / Morningstar /CNBC / Bloomberg / WSJ / Barron's / Motley Fool / TheStreet
- **Evaluate stocks**
  Finviz / SeekingAlpha / MSN Money / Zacks / Daily Finance / ADR / Fidelity / BlueChipGrowth / Earnings Impact / OpenInsider / NYSE / NASDAQ / SEC / SEC for 10K and 10Q (quarterly) reports required to file for listed stocks in major exchanges.
- **Charts**
  BigCharts / FreeStockCharts / StockCharts /
- **Screens**
  Yahoo!Finance / Finviz / CNBC / Morningstar /
- **Besides stocks**
  123Jump / Hoover's Online / FINRA Bond Market Data / REIT / Commodity Futures / Option Industry
- **Vendors**
  AAII / Zacks / IBD / GuruFocus / Vector Vest / Fidelity / Interactive Brokers / Merrill Lynch /
- **Economy.**
  Econday / EcoconStats / Federal Reserve / Economist /
- **Misc.**
  Dow Jones Indices / Russell / Wilshire / IRS / Wikinvest / ETF Database / ETF Trends / Nolo (estate planning) / AARP /

Appendix 4 - ETFs / Mutual Funds

What is an ETF

ETFs have basic differences from mutual funds: 1. Lower management expenses, 2. Trade ETFs same as stocks, and 3. Usually more diversified but not selective than the related mutual funds such as NOBL vs FRDPX.

The major classifications of ETFs are 1. Simulating an index such as SPY, QQQ and DIA, 2. Simulating a sector such as XLE and SOXX, 3. Simulating an asset class such as GLD and SLV, 4. Simulating a country or a group of countries such as EWC and FXI, 5. Managed by a manager(s) such as ARKK, 6. Betting a market or sector to go down such as SH and PSQ, and 7. Leveraged (not recommended for beginners).

Fidelity: Index ETFs (https://www.fidelity.com/etfs/overview).

Wikipedia on ETF (http://en.wikipedia.org/wiki/Exchange-traded_fund).

List of ETFs

ETF Bloomberg
http://www.bloomberg.com/markets/etfs/
ETF data base
http://etfdb.com/
ETF Trends
http://www.etftrends.com/
A list of ETFs. Seeking Alpha.
(http://etf.stock-encyclopedia.com/category/)

Fidelity's commission-free ETFs. Check current offerings and whether they are still commission-free.
(https://www.fidelity.com/etfs/ishares)

Fidelity Annuity funds with performance data.
http://fundresearch.fidelity.com/annuities/category-performance-annual-total-returns-quarterly/FPRAI?refann=005

A list of contra ETFs (or bear ETFs)
http://www.tradermike.net/inverse-short-etfs-bearish-etf-funds/

Misc.: ETFGuide, ETFReplay (highly recommended).

Other resources
Your broker should have a lot of information on ETFs and many offer commission-free ETFs.

Most subscription services offer research on ETFs. IBD has a strategy dedicated to ETFs and so does AAII to name a couple. Seeking Alpha has extensive resources for ETF including an ETF screener and investing ideas.

Not all ETFs are created equal
Check their performances and their expenses.

Small but well-performing ETFs
Here is a list.
http://finance.yahoo.com/news/small-etfs-pack-big-punch-195430875.html

Guggenheim Spin-Off ETF (CSD) looks interesting. The ETF tracks corporate spinoffs. It has beaten SPY for a long time; check the current performance. Not a recommendation.

When not to use ETFs
I prefer sector mutual funds in some industries but you need to do extensive research. They are drug industry, banks, miners and insurers.

Half ETF
Taking out half of the stocks that score below the average in an index ETF could beat the same full ETF itself. I call it HETF (half the ETF). You heard it here first.

To illustrate, sort the expected P/E (not including stocks with negative earnings) in ascending order and only include the stocks on the first half. Add more fundamental metrics. It will take a few minutes.

Disadvantages of ETFs
- When you have two stocks in a sector ETF one good one and one bad one, the ETF treats them the same. Stock pickers would buy the one that has a better appreciation potential.
- The return is better than the actual return due to stock rotation. To illustrate this, on August 29, 2012, SHLD was replaced by LYB in a sector fund. SHLD was down by 4% and LYB was up by 4% primarily due to the switch. Unless you sell and buy at the right time (which is impossible), your return would not match the ETF's returns due to the replacement.
- Ensure the performance matches the corresponding index, but will most likely not include dividends.

Advantages of ETFs
- We have demonstrated that you can beat the market by using market timing. Between 2000 and Nov., 2013, you only exit and reenter the market 3 times and the result is astonishing.
- It is easy to rotate a sector vs. buying/selling all of the stocks in this sector. It makes sector rotation the same as trading a stock.
- The risk is spread out and your portfolio is diversified especially for a market ETF or buying three or more ETFs in different sectors.
- Eliminate the time in researching stocks.

Leveraged ETFs
I do not recommend them. Some are 2x, 3x and even higher. They're too risky. However, when you are very sure or your tested strategy has very low drawdown, you may want to use them to improve performance. I recommend skipping all leveraged ETFs.

My basic ETF tables

I use a list of selected ETFs and commission-free (check the details) ETFs from Fidelity for my purpose. I include some mutual funds in Fidelity's annuity. Some of these may be interesting to you. I use ETFs for sector rotation and parking my cash when the market is favorable and I do not have stocks that I want to buy. ETFs and funds come and go. Some ideas and classifications are my own interpretation.

Table by market cap:

Category	ETF	Fidelity ETF	Mutual Funds	Fidelity's Annuity	Contra ETF
Size:					
Large Cap	DIA		See Blend		DOG
	SPY				SH
	QQQ	ONEQ			PSQ
	RYH				
Blend	IWD	IVV	BEQGX		
Growth	SPYG	IVW	FBGRX		
Value	SPYV		DOGGX		
Dividend	NOBL	DVY	FRDPX		
	VYM				
Mid Cap				FNBSC	MYY
Blend	MDY	JJH	VSEQX		
Growth		IJK	STDIX		
			BPTRX		
Value		IJJ	FSMVX		
Small Cap				FPRGC	SBB
Blend	IWM	IJR	HDPSX		
Growth		IJT	PRDSX		
Value		IJS	SKSEX		
Micro	IWC				
Multi					
Blend			VDEOX		
Growth			VHCOX		
Value			TCLCX		
Bond					
Long Term (20)	VLV		BTTTX		TBF
Mid Term (7 – 10)	VCIT		FSTGX		
Short Term (1 – 3 yrs.)	VCSH		THOPX		
Total	BOND		PONDX		
Corp Invest Grade	VCIT		NTHEX		
High Yield	PHB		SPHIX		

(junk)					
Muni	MUB		Check state		
Special situation					
Buy back	PKW				

Table by sectors:

Sector	ETF	Fidelity ETF	Mutual Funds	Fidelity's Annuity
Banking[1]			FSRBK	
Regional	IAT			
Bio Tech	IBB		FBIOX	
	XBI		Large	
Consumer Dis.	XLY	FDIS	FSCPX	FVHAC
Consumer Staple	XLP	FSTA	FDFAX	FCSAC
Finance	KIE	FNCL	FIDSX	FONNC
	IYF			
Energy	XLE	FENY	FSENX	FJLLC
Energy Service			FSESX	
Gold	GLD		FSAGX	
Gold Miner	GDX		VGPMX	
Health Care	IYH	FHLC	FSPHX	FPDRC
	VHT		VGHCX	
House Builder	ITB		FSHOX	
	ITB		Perform	
Industrial	IYJ	FIDU	FCYIX	FBALC
Material	VAW	FMAT	FSDPX	
	IYM			
Oil	USO			
Oil Service	OIH		FSESX	
Oil Exploration	XOP			
Real Estate	VNQ		FRIFX	FFWLC
REIT	VNQ			
Retail	RTH		FSRPX	
	XRT			
Regional bank	KRE		FSRBX	

Semi Conduct	SMH			
Software	XSW		FSCSX	
	IGV			
Technology	XLK	FTEC	FSPTX	FYENC
	FDN		FBSOX	
			ROGSX	
Telecomm.	VOX	FCOM	FSTCX	FVTAC
Transport	XTN			
	IYT			
Utilities	XLU	FUTY	FSUTX	FKMSC
Wireless			FWRLX	

Footnote. [1] Also check Finance.

Table by countries outside the USA:

Country	ETF	Fidelity ETF	Mutual Funds	Fidelity's Annuity
Australia	EWA			
Brazil	EWZ			
Canada	EWC		FICDX	
China	FXI		FHKCX	
EAFE	EFA			
Emerging	VWO		FEMEX	FEMAC
Europe	VGK		FIEUX	
Global	KXI		PGVFX	
Greece	GREK			
India	INDY		MINDX	
Indonesia	EIDO			
Latin America	ILF		FLATX	
Nordic			FNORX	
Hong Kong	EWH			
Japan	EWJ		FJPNX	
S. Africa	EZA			
S. Korea	EWY		MAKOX	
Singapore	EWS			
Taiwan	EWT			
Turkey	TUR			
United Kingdom	EWU			
Foreign:				
Combination	1	2	3	4
Intern. Div.	IDV	DWX		
Small Cap	SCZ	GWX		
Value	EFV			
Europe	VGK			

#Filler: Honey, my book can play music.
https://www.youtube.com/watch?v=HxGT5z6d-GA&list=PLMZa6mP7jZ2b1otqG4tfbgZpLEdh6YiNF
It may cut down commercials by casting it to TV.

www.ingramcontent.com/pod-product-compliance
Lightning Source LLC
Chambersburg PA
CBHW051909170526
45168CB00001B/309